SURRENDER
to
RISE

SURRENDER
to
RISE

Turning Fear and Struggle into Strength and Success

Elena Rodriguez

Denise Aguiar, Julie Loughlin Haers, Rossana Latham,
Jessica Montalvo, Melinda Heller, Brittany Buesching,
Dawn Rodriguez, Tish Ross

Xulon Press

Xulon Press
555 Winderley Pl, Suite 225
Maitland, FL 32751
407.339.4217
www.xulonpress.com

© 2024 by Elena Rodriguez

All rights reserved solely by the author. The author guarantees all contents are original and do not infringe upon the legal rights of any other person or work. No part of this book may be reproduced in any form without the permission of the author.

Due to the changing nature of the Internet, if there are any web addresses, links, or URLs included in this manuscript, these may have been altered and may no longer be accessible. The views and opinions shared in this book belong solely to the author and do not necessarily reflect those of the publisher. The publisher therefore disclaims responsibility for the views or opinions expressed within the work.

Paperback ISBN-13: 978-1-66289-353-7
Ebook ISBN-13: 978-1-66289-354-4

She continues to give to others when she's got nothing left for herself.
She hustles and grinds and does it afraid while the rest of the world silently sleeps.
She knows pure strength comes from complete surrender and so rejoices in the fall.
She loses count of the silent tears wiped away and continues to share her smile.
She beams of magnificence from a heart of pure gold and yet moves fiercely with a spirit of fire.
She cannot be stopped.
She will not quit.
She rises higher with each defeat.
She is a Comeback Queen
She is ME!

TABLE OF CONTENTS

INTRODUCTION: I CELEBRATE YOU IX
CHAPTER 1: PAINT YOUR SMILE 1
CHAPTER 2: STOP ASKING QUESTIONS 7
CHAPTER 3: THE COMEBACK BEGINS 11
CHAPTER 4: BREAKDOWN TO
             BREAKTHROUGH 15
CHAPTER 5: IT'S NEVER TOO LATE 27
CHAPTER 6: YOU ARE NOT UNGRATEFUL 37
CHAPTER 7: MY ROAD TO PEACE 51
CHAPTER 8: BELIEVE IN YOURSELF. 61
CHAPTER 9: BRAVE WOMAN. 69
CHAPTER 10: I AM NOT A STATISTIC 83
CHAPTER 11: DO WHAT MAKES YOU ROLL 91
CHAPTER 12: SECRET WITHIN 99
CONCLUSION: WALK IN FAITH 115

INTRODUCTION

I CELEBRATE YOU

HEY THERE, BEAUTIFUL, chances are if you are here, you have gone through some of life's hardest beatdowns. I'm not talking *Oops, I tripped and that hurt just a little bit* beatdown, I'm talking *Rocky in the ring taking punch after punch, refusing to be stopped* beatdown.

There's a difference. You are different because you could have quit many times, and you didn't. I know you have had to tap into tremendous strength to just keep living, and I know there are days you doubted if you could, or if you even wanted to. Trust me, I know.

But you did it! You found a way. You didn't give up. You kept going and you came back stronger, braver, more fierce and with a faith that can't be measured. You are a Comeback Queen and I honor you, I see you, I am you.

I am also taking this moment to celebrate you because you deserve it. Celebrate you because you could have quit, and you didn't. Celebrate you because you found a new way. Celebrate you because you picked up your broken pieces and started building a new dream. Celebrate you for choosing you.

I know the journey you have been on has not been easy, and my wish for you is that within these pages you will find the hope and inspiration to not only recognize and honor the powerhouse you are, but to also realize you are not alone.

We are Comeback Queens, afterall, and we are able to turn beatdowns into blessings and make our dreams come true.

Elena

CHAPTER 1

PAINT YOUR SMILE

❧❧❧

"When your lipstick is on point, people notice you" that's a line I use in my lipstick company today. You may be wondering what does lipstick have to do with *Surrender to Rise and Faith and God*?

Did you know God will use any avenue necessary to reach you if you are seeking Him? At times it may be hard to recognize His messages because they are often hidden in weird or odd places, and in my case, hidden in lipstick.

The key is staying open to receiving His messages wherever they may be placed, without question no matter how crazy or bazaar they seem. You see, for many years I didn't want to be seen because I could no longer genuinely find my smile and I grew tired of faking it. It was exhausting.

I had always been the bubbly person, the nice person, the one who was always there for others when needed, and I got along with everyone. I was always the leader, in charge, and the one people came to for advice and wisdom and guidance. Eventually, that all began to change.

I found myself hiding, isolating myself from friends and family. I gained weight and didn't like who I saw when I looked in the mirror. I was in a marriage that was very toxic and I don't throw that word around loosely. I walked on eggshells most days and awaited the "flip to switch" and the fights to begin and the apologizing to follow. I'd then patiently wait for the days to pass that were filled with the awkward and familiar silent treatment.

I walked around with this hovering anxiety and fear most days, and yet, painted a beautiful picture of a happy home full of love and joy…because ultimately, I believed I needed to love my husband better and in doing so, he would eventually love me better, too.

I prayed for strength to forgive more. I prayed for patience, for kindness and laughter. I prayed for him to stop looking at me like he hated me some days. I prayed for love. I just wanted to be loved and I thought if I did better, it would get better.

Have you ever gone about your days pretending they were *just peachy* only to find yourself growing smaller and smaller inside with each passing hour? Like, you can literally feel your spirit crying out, pleading for air, because it's being suffocated by everything and everyone around you.

That was me. I was screaming inside. My spirit was covered in so much darkness and it was slowly killing me from the inside out. I physically became ill. In one year I had four biopsies on four different parts of my body. I was sick. I was stuck. I was lost and I knew I was meant for more. This is not what God created me for, I thought. It just couldn't be. I was a good person. I was nice and kind and had faith strong enough to move mountains, and I knew this couldn't be it for me, but every time I tried to do more, I was shut down.

I began to feel stupid for believing I had a purpose, a calling on my life, and I'd fight within my own mind because a part of me knew I was meant for more, yet the other part didn't believe that silly lie at all. I would fall to my knees and cry in the shower because that was my safe space to feel free and just breathe, and I found comfort knowing the water would rinse my tears away without leaving a trace.

I began to pray harder and begged God to change my husband's heart. I would beg and plead to God and let Him know that I could feel I was being called to something great, but how would I get there in this dark dark place I was living? I remember telling God that I knew I didn't deserve anything, that I believed He only rewarded me for the work I did, but that I truly did not feel I deserved to be treated this way.

I would pray, *"Please change my husband's heart, my Lord Jesus, please change His heart so I can do the work you're calling me to do"* and He did. My husband had a heart attack and died on Christmas Eve.

Negativity is real, and it has the ability to destroy you. It nearly destroyed me. It can come at you in one big bomb that blows up your world, or it can slowly chip away at you, bit by bit, unrecognized until you one day look up and no longer recognize yourself. That's where I was, and on top of that, I was now a widow at 44 years old.

At that time, I thought my life had gotten the worst it could get. I wish I could tell you the hardest part was losing my husband, but I can't. It only kept going downhill from there. I had discovered I was living a life I knew nothing about, and I'm not even talking about the five year affair I discovered nine months after burying my husband, that was just the cherry on top. I had literally lost everything, including myself.

I had no money, no job, no dignity, no self-respect, no confidence, and no plan. All I had was a whole lot of faith, and although deep inside I knew that was enough, there were days I doubted if it really was. I held on though. It may have been with a very thin string but I held on to the knowing that even my moment of complete desperation held incredible purpose. I couldn't see it. I couldn't understand it, but I believed it.

I had reached a point in my life where there really wasn't anything left to lose and I really didn't have it in me to keep going, so I knew it was time. I had to surrender. I had to completely break down, tap out, and give everything to my G.O.D. (my Grand. Overall. Designer.) my Main Man, because I could not stand on my own anymore, I didn't want to. I was defeated. I was done. I was tired.

Have you ever been tired? Like tired tired. Like, the tired that sleep doesn't fix. The tired that says why even begin. The tired that believes none of it matters anyway. Yeah, I was tired.

So, I ended up living back at my mom's house, feeling like a complete failure. Failure as a daughter, failure as a mother, and failure as a woman. I just couldn't do it anymore. Healing through grief was hard but discovering an affair during my healing was just too much. I felt worthless, stupid, lost, broken, unloved, disregarded, like a piece of trash, and I just wanted to crawl in a hole and die myself.

But God doesn't work that way. God doesn't let anything go to waste, not even pain. God can turn anything around and make it great again, and so here's how lipstick saved me.

One evening, I was sitting on a recliner at my mom's house, having one too many glasses of wine, and scrolling through pictures having a grand ol' time at my private pity party. I came across a photo of myself from when I had a neck surgery the year prior. Even though I was in incredible physical pain in the photo, I still had my lipstick on and at that moment, something crazy happened to me, it's like God said "Here you go. Here's your chance to do something for you and turn your life around."

Have you ever had a really crazy idea? Well, this was one I was having and I didn't care because I needed fun in my life. I needed color back in my days and I needed something that was going to bring me joy, and as simple as it sounds, lipstick does that for me. For as long as I can remember, lipstick has always been the finishing piece that has pulled me together even when everything else in my world may have been falling apart.

...and so, right there on a recliner at my mom's house, after losing everything, feeling sorry for myself, wondering how I ended up "here" and not really wanting to go on anymore, my lipstick company was born.

Sure I was scared and I had no idea what I was doing or how to get started or who to go to for help, and sure people thought I was nuts when I said that I was going to start a lipstick line of my own, but you know what else happened?

I started waking up differently. Passion was once again burning inside of me. Fun was a part of my days again. I was surrounded by color and I started to really believe I could make a difference in a unique way again. I started to dream big and I had hope because I was no longer walking about my days in darkness, instead, I was now living in the light that God created just for me and I didn't feel alone anymore.

So, trust me when I say, I know how hard it is to find your smile some days because there were days I literally had to paint mine on. "Paint Your Smile" is my personal message to you that comes from knowing the effort and strength it takes to smile while everything hurts.

Wherever you find yourself today, know this, it will get better. You are given something unique and special so never think all the good stuff is only for them, it's for you. God is always with you and never leaves you. He is THAT BIG that if you simply reach for Him, you will not miss.

CHAPTER 2

STOP ASKING QUESTIONS

"STOP WASTING PRECIOUS time asking questions you know you will never receive answers to." This one single sentence and those few simple words, changed my life. They will change yours too if you let them. You see, we all have those questions in our life. The ones that are on repeat some days and no matter how many times you ask them, no matter how many clever variations you can come up with, the answer is still the same...there is no answer.

God reminded me of this when I continued to beat myself up after the discovery of my husband's affair. I would ask, over and over again, "why" or "what did I do wrong" or "what could I have done differently" or "what could I have done better" or "why wasn't I enough" or "did I cause this" or "was this my fault" and He finally just said "STOP."

I was reminded at that very moment that no matter how many times I asked, wondered, whispered, shouted, or cried out, it didn't matter, I was never going to get an answer because my husband was dead. God reminded me that my precious time was being wasted. Precious time that could be spent rebuilding a life of happiness and love. Precious time creating new memories and laughter with my kids. Precious time doing what I love...building my dream and doing whatever my heart desired and whatever God continued to call me to do!

I don't know what you want to do with your precious time, but I must ask, "Are you wasting it?" Let that question sink in a bit, are you wasting your precious time asking questions you know you will never receive answers to? It can be eye opening, at least I know it was for me.

It doesn't have to take someone dying for you to be left with unanswered questions. I bet, right now, you can think of a few questions you ask yourself again and again that truly have no answers. How different will your life look if you just stop asking questions and instead use that time to do something with the unique gifts God has given only to you.

God has fully equipped you to live a life that brings you pure joy, and what I've come to learn is that pure joy can only be experienced by living close to Him. Pure joy doesn't mean perfect and it doesn't mean living without pain and worry. Pure joy simply means that you recognize and honor the warm fuzzy feeling that fills your whole body up from top to bottom because you know it is coming from God's love and that makes everything better. With God's love, there is nothing you can't face and I'm a firm believer that God always gives us more than we can handle because we weren't meant to handle everything on our own.

I will never know why I had to go through all the beat-downs I've gone through, just as you may never know why you've had to go through your own, but I do trust that it's our job to do something positive with them. I do trust that as long as we lead with love and pure intentions, God will take care of the rest. I don't believe we get bonus points just because we do something good and I don't believe we get points taken away when we do something bad. I believe God loves us the same day after day and that is the driving force that keeps me pushing to do my best.

My motto is "Do everything with a spirit of excellence unto Him and you can't go wrong." For this reason, God uses me as a vessel, and is the reason you are here now, and so, brings us to this moment that I'm honored to share with you.

During my healing journey, my Surrender to Rise and Comeback journey, God shared this message with me, He said:

> Remember Who You Are
> Remember Whose You Are
> Boldly Step Forward
> Show Your Crown

These few words immediately did many things for me simultaneously. They made me feel safe, secure and they made me strong and courageous. They let me know I was seen, loved, and I was here for impact. They made me know I mattered, and that's why I share them with you, because you matter too.

So, honestly, I don't know what these words do for you but I do hope it's something grand.

Over the next several chapters you are going to hear from Comeback Queens who I have known for quite some time and who have impacted my life in tremendous ways.

Who I love and believe in. Who inspire me every day. Who are worthy of greatness and have endured much in their own lives. Who have lessons to teach and wisdom to share.

It is my hope that throughout these next personal stories of triumph, you will be inspired to share your story of your own. I know you have one.

I know you have endured much. You have overcome many obstacles that no one even knows about. That you have carried pain behind your own smile and at times have wondered what it's all been for.

I know at times it can be hard to see the gift in the pain but what I do know is this...

Even though it took death for me to truly start living, that it took betrayal for me to see my own beauty, that it took excruciating pain in becoming a widow to discover that I am not alone, I still trust, God does not make mistakes.

Yes, God does not make mistakes, and He doesn't want you to waste your precious time asking questions you know you will never receive answers to.

Simply, take care of your minutes, and your days, weeks, years will take care of themselves. Trust me...it's beautiful.

CHAPTER 3

THE COMEBACK BEGINS

ONE OF THE questions I still get asked often after all these years is, "Elena, how did you make your comeback?" I have to be honest with you, this used to be a very strange question to me because I wondered, *Where did I go? Where did I come back from? I've always been here...but have I really?*

As I have thought about this question again and again, it dawned on me that it really isn't about how I made my comeback; it's about how I found the strength to keep going on.

People really wanted to know how I found positivity in every moment of devastation, how I was able to pray for the women who had a five year affair with my husband, how I was able to rebuild financially after losing all my money, how I was able to start a business from the recliner at my mom's house after losing my home, how I was able to strengthen my relationship with my boys after feeling like a failure as a mother, and how I was able to build new levels of confidence after my self-esteem was destroyed and my heart ripped to shreds.

Yeah, that infamous question isn't about how I made my comeback, it's really about the need for support and encouragement from those who refuse to give up on themselves, yet don't know where to begin.

I've thought long and hard about this thing called *the comeback* and it comes down to one word for me, one place of beginning: SURRENDER. The moment you realize you have very little control over anything in this life is the moment true power becomes yours.

Respecting the simple fact that not even the moment you will take your very last breath here on earth is in your control releases the high demands of expectations you place on yourself. This, my friend, is the moment you gain divine freedom and it's within this new found place of divine freedom that your spirit begins to thrive as God intended it to all along.

My moment of Surrender was both my weakest and strongest moments happening together in unison for my greater good. It's like fear and love decided to work together because they knew it's what I needed to live. My place of surrender removed the immense pressure of survival I had been carrying and I was able to experience everything from a new perspective. I was able to see myself through God's eyes and no longer from the shame that darkened mine. It was a beautiful experience and I want to share how the gift of surrender is one that you can also receive.

Making the choice to surrender is not an easy one. It doesn't come naturally and most times only comes when you are put in a position where you feel there is nothing else you can do. When you find yourself at this breaking point you are faced with two choices:

One, to keep holding tight, keep pushing, keep fighting, keep resisting, keep hiding, keep lying to yourself and trying to figure it out on your own.

Or two, let God know you are giving it all to Him…and then Let.It.Go.

Surrender looks different for each of us. It happens in different ways and at different speeds and there is no right or wrong way. As you read phenomenal comeback stories from amazing women, I hope you will see yourself in them. I hope you will realize how resilient you are and how powerful you are and that you are not alone in your own personal journey of healing.

I have put together 9 Key Elements that make Surrender the most powerful force in your life. You will read true examples of how the power of surrender showed up in the lives of other women, including myself.

As you read these chapters, I ask that you start dreaming again. Begin believing in yourself on a deeper level and trusting that the best days of your life are on their way to you right now. Trust that blessings already have your name written all over them and are waiting for you to claim them, and know you are here to make a difference and that you matter. Understand that this moment in your life is the beginning of something magnificent and so...The Comeback Begins!

CHAPTER 4

BREAKDOWN TO BREAKTHROUGH

SURRENDER to RISE
S-Surrender

Chapter written by Denise Aguiar

Acknowledgements: I give thanks to my parents for bringing me into the world. Had it not been for them, I would not be here today. To my son Demy, you are the reason I am who I am today. You give me strength and put things into perspective. You help me wake my inner child and smell the roses.

Loving ourselves through the process of owning our story is the bravest thing we'll ever do. — Brene Brown

I USED TO be very self-conscious and a perfectionist who had to be in control of my every move. I used to daydream a lot and think about who I wanted to be and all I wanted to accomplish, until I mentally collapsed and had a nervous breakdown. Let me take you back for a moment...

Where It All Begins

Do not despise small beginnings... – Zechariah 4:10

It all started in January 1975. My mother gave birth to me in the Republic of Cape Verde in West Africa. My great grandmother, whom everyone called Mamãe, helped my mother and father raise me and my brother until I was about five years old.

When we were living in Cape Verde, I remember going to a daycare center, and I loved it when my father came to pick me up. My father was my world. I remember the first time my father went on a business trip to Portugal and he brought back a radio. This radio became a huge part of our family time in our household.

My life in Cape Verde was short lived. My parents decided it would be best to move to Portugal because it was closer to where my father did his work. The hardest part of moving to

Portugal was leaving my Mamãe behind. She was my everything and took such good care of me and all the kids in the village. My parents felt that moving to Portugal was the best option to raise me and my brother, who was deaf. A few years later my two younger brothers were born while we lived in Portugal.

For the next 10 years, Amadora, a small city outside of Lisbon, Portugal, became my home. It is the place I still consider my hometown. I eventually saw moving to Portugal as the best thing because it was there I met my childhood best friends Rita, Natasha, Teresa, Suzanna, and Pedro.

Growing up I always thought we were financially rich, but we were rich in culture. As I've gotten older, I feel blessed to have grown up in a home with so much love from my father, my mother, and my three brothers. My dad often traveled for work and always brought us something back. Once he brought me a red headed doll. She was my favorite doll for the longest time until one of my female cousin's decided to color her face with markers.

My mother was a serious woman who protected her loved ones. She would go out of her way if she felt that any of her loved ones and friends were not being treated well. I remember one time she marched to a nearby grocery store to give the store owner a piece of her mind because one of her friends had not been treated fairly. That's the kind of woman my mother was—a protector of weak souls. Whenever we had family or guests at our home, she was ready to do whatever it took to make sure they were taken care of.

In 1989, at the tender age of 36, my mother passed away from a brain hemorrhage. I was just 14 at the time. As my mother was dying, my father didn't allow my brothers and I to see her in the hospital. Although I have forgiven him, I still don't understand his motive or reason for not letting us say our good-byes. My father said she was not in the best condition to receive us. I will never know how true that was, but I have no choice but to believe him.

Growing up my father was my hero, but after my mom passed away our relationship changed dramatically. I felt it was his fault that my mom was gone. My father is a complicated man to understand. Like most men I've known, he keeps things bottled inside. It was at this point that my life started to change. A few months after her death, we moved to the United States, or the Dream Land as we called it.

My father, as I said earlier, was my hero but a few weeks after my mother passed away and right before we moved to the United States something changed.

I was taking a bath and my father got in the tub with me scaring the crap out of me. I ran out the tub as fast as I could because I was no longer a little girl. My reaction was triggered from a previous experience from when we first arrived in Portugal. We had lived for a while at my uncle's house where he molested me and would tell me not to tell a soul because if I did, we would not have a place to live.

Needless to say, I was overjoyed when we moved to our home in Amadora because I was free from the scum bag that took advantage of my soul, so I was not about to experience that with my father. Maybe my father was not going to do anything, but like I said, I was not a little girl anymore.

My mom was my best friend. When she departed this Earth, I lost a big chunk of me, so did my brothers, especially my deaf brother because she was the one that protected him. Her death was such a hard loss. I still miss her to pieces to this day. She was my source of love, and my strength. It is because of her and my past that I am who I am today. I often imagine myself as achieving success for both my mother and me. She is and will always be my first love.

Taking Off the Mask

> *Nothing can dim the light that shines from within.*
> *-Maya Angelou*

So here I am today, all grown up, and a lot has happened. A few years back, I had what's known as a psychotic episode. I was unable to sleep for six days straight. Our last move was extra hard as I was suffering from insomnia and anxiety, and my then husband had to be away within days of us moving into our new home.

I wanted to stay longer in the hotel before moving into our new home, but my ex-husband and kids liked our new house. My ex-husband pressured our move without considering my feelings.

Like everyone else, he saw me as the strong and determined woman who always accomplished everything, but this time it was different.

On this particular day as my ex-husband departed; my anxiety was at an all-time high. I began hallucinating to the point that I couldn't tell reality from fantasy. By the time he returned, I was really struggling. It was like I was on high and no one could stop me from going.

Everything came to a head on a Thursday afternoon when my stepson had a medical appointment. After the appointment, we ran some errands, and at first, we were having a great time in the car. We were having so much fun that we missed a turn and became lost. My phone was acting up, so I couldn't get GPS to work.

Finally, after a few minutes, I got hold of my ex-husband who tried to give directions because apparently, we had driven far. I was getting frustrated because the cars behind me were honking their horns. I was going slower than the speed limit. I was trying to keep the little sanity that I still had under control.

Eventually we pulled over to wait for my ex-husband to guide us back home. The car needed gas, so I stopped at the first gas station I saw. I sent my stepson inside to get a snack because we were starving. My ex-husband didn't like that we had to stop.

I went inside to sit down for a bit while my stepson picked his snack. My husband became impatient and raised his voice. He yelled, " Hurry the hell up!" That's all it took for me to snap.

I told my ex-husband to chill out in my loudest voice. I was already starting to show signs of a nervous breakdown. I asked him to call my ride-or-die, Kim. He suggested we wait until we get home, but I wasn't having it. I ran to the restrooms and locked myself inside. I told him I would not get out until I spoke to Kim or my son, Demy. I even shouted at him to buy a ticket for Demy and I to go to the U.S. It got crazy and loud.

Finally, I spoke to Kim. I could barely hear her voice in the midst of my sobbing. I returned the phone to my ex-husband, then I took off my shoes and took off running. I felt tired and hopeless. I hid behind a bush where I threw my wedding ring, a few coins, and a bracelet.

I felt tired, and even though I knew my ex-husband and stepson were looking for me, I just laid on the wet pavement and closed my eyes. I didn't get up until I heard my stepson call my name. That's when I ran from my hiding spot and almost got hit by a German police car.

This episode is the real reason I decided to share my story, my struggles, and my battles.

Finally, everything came out. I had wrestled with adjustment disorder for some time.

Looking back, I always went through something similar every time I moved from place to place, especially during my time in the military.

I was eventually diagnosed with generalized anxiety disorder, adjustment disorder and depression, and since my diagnosis, I have learned that anxiety disorder is a condition, and not a disease.

After 20 years of searching for answers to my constant anxiety, I finally had a name for my struggle. Before I was able to keep a mask on, but after moving twelve times, the pain became too unbearable.

Looking back, I guess I have always had underlined anxiety, and it reached its peak while I was working at the US Embassy in Qatar. I was faced with a toxic leader, a challenging subordinate, and what felt like a "huge" Inspection at the time, all which would test my leadership skills and the many hats I wore.

Anxiety disorder is characterized by feelings of "extra" fear of the unknown and mood swings. The intensity of the symptoms can vary from mild to extreme. According to my psychiatrist, I am in the mild spectrum, though when it comes to anxiety, I feel lost more times than I wish upon anyone.

It has become a daily effort for me to have a good handle on my anxiety. I give thanks for the wonders of medicine that keep my nervous system intact. Routine, fitness, and meditation are equally important to keep my nervous system regulated.

Meditation has quieted my soul and mind, but it wasn't easy at first because I just couldn't bring myself to focus only on my breath or a word. My mind wandered more times than I desired and I felt an overwhelming sense of panic (anxiety). But then one day it clicked. I learned that by allowing my mind to wander it allowed me to let it be, and quietly refocus my attention back to the present moment.

It didn't happen overnight and at times I just wanted to throw my hands in the air and find other alternatives, but since I am not a quitter I didn't give up. It took practice.

If you are wondering if meditation can help you, I am here to tell you to give it a go, be patient and try it for one minute, three minutes, five minutes and eventually you will be able to meditate for longer than 15 minutes. I promise you. I have come to accept that anxiety is the fear of the unknown.

My medications have done wonders for my mental status (side note: one of the side effects is weight gain…ugh, but since writing this chapter I have changed meds and I am "somewhat" more in control of my weight).

As long as the symptoms are mild, depression remains undiagnosed. In my case, therapy has also helped. I was blessed to have a good psychologist and psychiatrist. Through therapy I learned that although I seem strong, I was storing a lot of unwanted baggage which needed to be dealt with.

Have a support system in place. When I am dealing with my struggles, my best friend Kim is the first to know because I want someone that understands my pain. There's lots of shame with mental illness because no one wants to be judged or placed in a category that is still considered taboo.

When I tried to come out and share my inner struggles with family and friends, I was not taken seriously until I had my first maniac moment. This incident has changed my life.

I have decided to be real about who I am and not worry about what others think of me.

I am blessed to be here because during my maniac moment all I wanted to do was to die, let go of the pain inside, and not be a burden to others. I have decided that from now on, I will be the person I am meant to be without a mask.

Live life beyond your fears, don't be afraid to seek mental help. Let's break the mental health stigma.

I am who I am and I don't regret any of the rough waters I've had to go through because they made me stronger, more independent, more assertive and to know what it's like to achieve true happiness, which continues to be a work in progress.

Through my story, I hope that you will take my experiences and be inspired to live your own life beyond your fears.

BREAK THE MENTAL HEALTH STIGMA!

Prayers from Elena:

As Denise shared her story about her mental health struggle, and her moment of breakdown, can we please take a moment and pray over her, and anyone else who struggles with mental health challenges?

Lord Jesus, may you place your Hands of Peace over Denise and those who battle mental health issues. May you calm anxiety before it surfaces and may you allow understanding, patience, and compassion to those who care for those with mental health issues as it can sometimes be difficult to comprehend. May you provide strength and healing over the bodies and minds of all those impacted by these issues.

In your name...
Amen

CHAPTER 5

IT'S NEVER TOO LATE

SURRENDER to RISE
U-Unconditional Love

Chapter written by Julie Loughlin Haers

Acknowledgements: To my hero, my heart, my everything, my son Jared. You are and will always be the reason I work as diligently as I do. You inspire me everyday to be a better person and I know that God chose me to be your mom to show me unconditional, true, and pure love. I will always be your number one fan. Thank you for being the best son to a mom that wanted you more than anything.

I'm married but I feel completely alone, "How can this be?"

THIS IS NOT going to get better...He is not going to change! These thoughts ran through my mind as I stood in line at the airport, embarrassed in front of a line full of people as we headed to Florida for vacation.

Instead of being excited about our vacation, I was being yelled at, by my then husband, to get out of the way "I know what I'm doing" he said, when I was the one that packed all the bags, I was the one who knew where the nebulizer was. I knew what was making the bag heavy. But again, why would he miss the opportunity to embarrass me, he never missed one before.

I thought he heard what I said when I told him "*If* I were to come back, I needed to be treated with kindness and respect". Then it happened again. The flashbacks all came rushing back to me, the times he discounted me and didn't value me. In that very moment in 2010 I finally chose "Me". I can't stay in this marriage, not for him, not for my family and toughest of all not even for my son. If I don't honor what I need and show my son that I don't accept this behavior, what will he be like in the future?

I was done with all the "hiding of assets and not knowing the full story on anything financially" in our marriage. He was constantly spending large sums of money on high ticket items that I did not know about or even agree to. Meanwhile, he expected me to tie up all my income in maintaining our household to the point where I couldn't even save for retirement. I was completely fed up. He had promised he'd make changes on three major areas, and he had not made one change. I no longer could tolerate our situation. I had never felt more alone in my life than I did in these moments. I'm married but I feel completely alone, "How is this?"

Something inside of me snapped and I decided I'm leaving and this time I am not coming back. I got very intentional and created a plan to create the life I wanted with my son. I knew I would never be able to maintain the home we had built together, I also knew he would try his best to not have to pay child support or alimony. I just knew him. So, I found a townhouse in my hometown as a rental, and I moved out. I needed space to reconnect with myself and create a nice environment for me and my son.

I worked incredibly hard Monday-Wednesday traveling as an independent new business development manager for various brands. It was the type of job that required me to be face to face with my business owner clients. I was able to be with my son Thursday to Monday and that is what our agreement reflected. I would often work 13-hour days to be able to get back to my home area by Thursday to pick my son up in the afternoon. I always looked forward to every Thursday.

In fact, my son is what kept me going through some of the darkest times of my life. As I reflect, I know that him being here is my true miracle as I had a team of expert doctors tell me "You will never carry a pregnancy to full term…" but they didn't know me. I knew that God put the dream of my child in my heart for a reason, I knew that he was meant to be here in this time and space, and I refused to give up on my dream of being a mom.

I went through 2 horrific miscarriages, one of which was a pregnancy that almost killed me. It took a huge toll on me. It was by far the hardest time of my life, Emotionally and physically. I had to have my blood drawn every other day 7 days a week for 3 months consistently. Literally all the veins in my arms and hands collapsed. The phlebotomist and I became good friends. After a few weeks, he said to me "Where is your husband?" and I just shook my head and cried.

During all these blood draws, all the needles and pokes, all the fighting to keep me and our child alive, which didn't happen, he never came. I was in deep despair. I would have my blood drawn, go out to my car and just cry. But I had no time to grieve. My ex-husband had convinced me that I could not take time off and that if I did, we would go backwards financially.

The collective toll that this took on me changed me. Because I had no one to really rely on, I got good at connecting with God and myself and I grew stronger every day.

I needed to create a safe space for myself and my son. I wanted to be in control of all my variables: where we lived, what we ate, how we spent my money, where we went on vacation. All of it. I wanted control. I no longer wanted it to be just about one person as it had been for 10 years. As my son got older, I would let him choose one vacation a year and I would choose one vacation. It was a collaboration, where each of us felt loved and valued.

After 2 years of a lot of back and forth we finally settled our divorce. I was physically, mentally and emotionally exhausted. I was able to find a job where I could come off the road for about a year. My income dropped significantly but I felt that my son and I needed this time together.

In March, 2021, we were eventually able to buy our own house and I was able to provide my son with a big room. I eventually realized that to create the kind of lifestyle that allowed me to solely provide for my son when he was with me, I would need to make more money. I started to travel again for work because it was what I knew, and I had convinced myself that any local job would not come close to the six figures plus range that I knew I needed to be in to be able to live the life we wanted.

I started traveling again and I was so good at business development that the company I was working with gave me one of the biggest territories and I had to fly to Texas at least twice a month from New York.

On my son's 7th birthday, I had to fly to San Antonio, Texas. I had pushed my departure time back as far as I could, and I did not leave until 4:00 pm that day, but it meant I had to be at the airport by 3:00pm at the latest. My parents and I took my son to a fun birthday lunch then to the toy store to pick out fun toys, but eventually we had to go to the airport.

My dad got out of the car to give me my carry on bag from the trunk and to see me off. I gave my son a huge hug and kiss and told him "I will be back in two days and we will have a fun birthday weekend" as tears were welling up in my eyes.

I was trying my best to be strong – I had no choice, this was my territory and I had to go to present at a huge client event.

My son started crying "Mommy, this is our special day together, I don't want you to go!" It literally broke my heart. I said "I know, and I love you and you will have so much fun with your grandparents, and I will be right back."

My dad handed me my bag and walked me to the airport door, at this point tears were streaming down my face, and he said to me, "Julie, please don't take this the wrong way. Your mom and I are so proud of the amazing, strong business person and single mom that you are, but this *–signaling over to my son–* this is so hard for you both, maybe it is time for you to rethink your career! I know you are so smart you could do anything, why not consider opening your own business like I did."

My father had opened a consulting company at age 50 after working for a large corporation for years and was extremely successful. My dad's words rang in my ears all the way to Texas and back. I was like he is right, it is time for the change.

I was beginning to realize that when God wants to get your attention, he will send messages through other people that you love and respect, and my dad was definitely that person for me.

The following weekend I was at the grocery store getting food for my son and I for the weekend and I ran into my high school best friend. We were ecstatic to see each other, like hugging and jumping up and down in the aisle, ecstatic. It had been years since we'd seen each other, but also somehow seemed like no time had passed. We made plans to meet that weekend with our kids to play in the park and for us to catch up.

She looked so amazing and seemed so very happy. She was a mom to a beautiful little girl and a wife to an amazing guy and I was so happy for her. As the kids were playing, we updated each other on our lives since high school. At one point she looked at me and said I prayed I would reconnect with you. I was so flattered by that comment.

She continued and said, "Julie, you were always the go-to person in high school to help people out of situations. You always gave great advice!" She took a deep breath, and she said "I need your help."

I said, "Anything, you name it!"

Her face changed to one of a lot of worry and I could not imagine what she was going to say next. She said to me, "I am sick. It is cancer, and it is extremely aggressive."

My heart sank but I did not let her see any of that.

She said, "I am like at a crossroads."

I told her, "I am RIGHT HERE WITH YOU and I will fight with you, right alongside of you." She looked at me and she said, "Thank you I need that right now."

And so we did, we fought, she and I. Her whole family, we all fought like hell. It was one of the most epic battles I had ever been in. It is with a heavy heart I share with you that my beautiful most loving friend lost her battle with cancer.

As I was with her for the last year and half of her life it was a massive gift to me. She PUSHED me and she motivated me. She taught me that life has a sense of urgency to it. She encouraged me to leave my big corporate job and start my own company helping people make good decisions. She said to me, "Julie, go for it and never look back. The world needs you. You can make a difference in the lives of others, as you have for me." She said, "Live your life to the fullest and do not play small."

I did exactly that in 2018. I left that big corporate job and throughout the past five years I have built my business, client by client.

I can share this with you today, with great joy, that I am grateful for all the hard days I went through. I am able to use all of what I went through, all my tough experiences, to help my clients use their financial resources in a way that honors the way they want to live now, and in the future.

I build plans that are in alignment with my clients desires. As I reflect, I realize now my whole life was preparing me for the role I play today as the Co-founder and Co-owner of Breathe Capital Planning.

I am grateful for every lesson because it is never too late to be who you always wanted to be.

PRAYERS FROM ELENA:

As Julie shared her story about losing her friend while finding what matters most in life, which is Unconditional Love, she encourages us, especially as powerful women, to step back and look at the value of living in the moment. Having overcome a broken marriage and devastation, she remained strong for her son. Something we can relate to and know does not come easy. Can we please take a moment and pray over her, and anyone else who struggles with broken relationships, and having to make difficult choices between career and parenting? It's not easy to have to wear all the hats and make sacrifices for the sake of holding together a single household.

Lord Jesus, may you share your Unconditional Love and Wisdom and Guidance over Julie and her son, and may you mend the broken hearts who walk around day after day feeling lost and broken. May you fill the scars that remain, both seen and unseen, with the abundance of your healing grace and allow joy to be felt under the blanket of your love over all who need you on this day.

In your name...
Amen

CHAPTER 6

YOU ARE NOT UNGRATEFUL

SURRENDER to RISE
R-Recognize

Chapter written by Rossana Latham

Acknowledgements: I would like to thank my G.O.D for the strength to be here and the ability to learn and grow stronger, physically, mentally, and emotionally. Also, I thank my friend, Elena Rodriguez, for the opportunity, guidance, and support to share my story and learning experience. And, last but not least, I wish the reader to believe in and recognize their own strengths, their capacity to love, and their ability to forgive themselves, first.

I would sit down and think of what I wanted to accomplish next with my life, now that I was free

YOU DO NOT OWE YOUR LIFE, SUCCESS OR HAPPINESS TO ANYONE. YOU ARE NOT UNGRATEFUL.

LET ME TELL you how I spent 20 years of my life thinking that I was doing the right thing by staying in a relationship where I always felt that I owed someone my life, my success, and my happiness, and why I felt that way.

I thought that I needed to keep it together because I needed to be grateful for all that I had, for the great opportunity I was given. I was a prisoner of my marriage, I locked myself in it, and became bitter and resentful. But, why?

My story starts back in 1998, when the Internet was booming with chat rooms, and finally, we could meet and talk with strangers online in chat room applications. I met many people, but struck a friendship with a young man who was very polite, down to earth and handsome. We would talk about our daily lives, family, relationships, exchanged care packages by mail, and eventually met in person.

Long story short, we liked each other enough and decided to marry.

I was in college, had one year left to finish my Engineering degree, but my new American boyfriend wanted me by his side as soon as possible. So, I dropped everything, including my degree, and moved to the USA.

Next thing you know, we are living together, getting married, and filing immigration paperwork that I paid for myself. I was eventually able to find work. He helped me find a car that I made payments on. I didn't have to pay house related bills, but I did have to pay for my own things, including doctor appointments.

I think I loved him and I think he loved me.

I was thinking, we are fine, we get along, we are young, we have fun with what little we have. Less than five years into this marriage, I noticed a change in the way I was being treated.

I was being called names, my opinion didn't matter. Here are some excerpts from my journal, to be more explicit, and to tell you exactly what was going through my head and my heart at that time:

"He calls me psycho when I tell him how I feel or think about him. He says that I am acting psycho for telling him that he should pick up the kitchen mess after making bread or cooking something. While I am telling him that, I am the one actually picking up the dirty stuff and cleaning the kitchen counter. Instead of helping, he tells me I am a psycho."

That day, he went off to take a shower, and instead of saying Thank You for cleaning the kitchen, he went to watch TV and told me to get off his back and leave him alone. We continually fought over leaving his dirty clothes laying around the dinner table chairs, the floors. But, I was called the messy one because after a while, I stopped picking up after his messes.

He didn't like to hear the truth about himself and needed to call me names and bring my morale down so he could feel better about himself.

Five years passed by and throughout that time, I was being called stupid all the time. My husband had no patience and had a very short temper with me. He'd mostly ask for help to do things related to his hobbies, I would be yelled at while helping, without being given any special instructions. He expected me to be able to read his mind or innately understand what he wanted me to do, and I had to do it right based on the expectations he had. Expectations which he failed to express to me before I started helping him with these activities.

Each episode ended with me leaving, crying, insulted, and feeling diminished; yes, feeling stupid.

Some days I feared I would be physically struck. I'd walk away to remove myself from the situation. My husband never apologized for his aggressions, for hurting my feelings. It was all okay with him.

Over the years, more little things that added to the aggressive behavior and unkind treatments towards me, got worse and I won't bore you with them all but it's safe to say, they didn't get any nicer.

At this point, I was sure I did not belong in this relationship. And, I started to wonder, why, if I am so stupid, why hasn't he traded me for someone who is not stupid, or nagging, or a psycho?

We all know there are two sides to every story. I am sure if you ask anyone about me, they would say I am kind, well mannered, fair, educated, and respectful. Even if my husband thought that my comments were not to his liking, there was still no reason to be disrespectful with the name calling, to be aggressive with his words of choice, and to put me in a situation where I would have to yell to make my point, express my feelings, or defend myself.

I am not a perfect person, but I am always trying to be better. I apologize for my mistakes and try to make rational decisions.

Throughout this time, I worked hard to grow professionally, I studied and finished 2 degrees, and tried to keep the house as livable as possible for a busy working household. I expressed my thoughts and feelings to my husband about how he treated me. All I got was: "That's how I am. I learned it from my dad."

Now, I will tell you, I spent more years waiting for him to change since he had made me aware of why he was the way he was. That day never arrived. I lost myself in the process and focused on work and my education.

I let myself go, gained weight, and was in emotional survival mode constantly. I did not feel any kind of affection towards my husband, I did not want to be hugged or touched or kissed. I was resentful all the time. It was not apparent, and I did not admit it until 15 years later.

I spent the next 5 years trying to catch up with myself, and laying the groundwork to regain my self-confidence and independence.

The last straw was when he confronted me for trying to better myself. He accused me of having an affair. With almost 20 years in the book, I decided it was time to say the words: "I want a divorce." I moved out 2 months later in the Fall of that year.

I waited and held back from leaving him earlier because I felt that I owed him for the opportunity he gave me to make a life in this country. I stayed because I thought that I had to be a good woman and be grateful and not complain. I stayed because I thought I had to be supportive and help him be a better person and change for good.

Truth is my now ex-husband is a good, kind, respectful, and successful person, he was just not that kind and respectful to me because of whom I represented in his life. Or, at least, that is what I believe.

Now, after I separated and divorced from my marriage, and found my way towards healing, I have learned about myself and why others might be the way they are and why they do the things they do and say. I like to learn from my experiences, and this is definitely something to learn from.

I don't try to make excuses for anyone, I just try to make sense of the whole situation, so I can heal and move on with my life.

Let's talk about generational trauma and a few other things. I had never heard of the term "generational trauma" before. I only learned about it after I started to speak with my life coach and read about toxic relationships.

Generational trauma is something passed down from generation to generation, also called intergenerational trauma. Traumas are caused by distressful events and situations in someone's life.

It becomes a generational trauma when the same fears or behaviors are passed down to someone in the next generation and so on, perhaps not in the same way the original distressful event happened, but behaviorally or by constant reminder to the next person.

Similarly, historical and cultural trauma are passed down generationally.

I believe that everyone has some percentage of generational trauma passed down from parents or grandparents, in addition to their own self-experiences that have reinforced such trauma. The topic of generational trauma is getting a lot of attention these days, studies are being conducted, but historically, the most studied events are those that involve large numbers of individuals affected by extremely traumatic events such as the Holocaust, African-American mistreatment, and foreign countries victims of war, for example.

Go ahead and read about it. It is a very interesting topic to learn about. On one of my visits to family back in Panama, I learned about my own generational trauma. I learned that at least one side of my family has a history of experiencing child neglect, emotional and verbal abuse, and even physical aggression when they were children.

Although I do not remember being treated the same way very early in my childhood, I do remember experiencing emotional and verbal abuse allowed by one of my parental units from their romantic partner.

We were told that we were worthless, that we were garbage and needed to be thrown away in bags. We were told that we had to earn our food and had to work for it. My parental unit chose her love life over her children.

We learned to live quietly, without speaking up because it didn't matter, and we were not taught about learning our true value. Without learning our true value, my brothers and I struggled during our early adult years. We have gone through depression, alcohol abuse, suicide attempts, anger issues, self-loathing, very poor self-esteem. My brothers and I experienced verbal and emotional abuse for about 10 years, until my parental unit and the partner moved out. I was already a young adult and could work to pay house bills at that time.

For me in particular, being aware of the family history of trauma, helps me understand that not knowing my true value has led me into not making the best choices for relationships. I did not have a good role model for that; my father died early in my childhood. The one adult male that was present when I was a child was verbally and emotionally abusive. Therefore, it seems that I unconsciously attract or feel attracted to men that have similar traits, behaviors, and eventually end up treating me the same way.

My personality tries to give them hope and give them opportunities to change or want to help them change, but that never happens. The change doesn't happen because it is not my job to fix anyone, especially if they do not want to be fixed, or changed.

In my ex-husband's case, all I know is that the father treated his wife with disrespect and that is how my ex-husband learned how to treat his wife, me. I understand that he had no choice on how he learned to treat a wife, but I do not agree that he needed to continue the behavior. I asked him to try to be better, but it never happened. He did not care if he hurt my feelings, if I cried and walked out mad or sad, or if I told him to stop being so mean to me or anyone he supposedly cared about. I did not want to be loved that way anymore.

When I moved out and into a tiny old house, I thanked God for friends and family who helped me strip the place down, clean, and paint the walls and ceilings. I had a ton of boxes cluttered in the tiny living room. In between putting things away, I would sit down and think of what I wanted to accomplish next with my life, now that I was free and had nobody to hurt me at home. Of course, I decided to do one of the things I was told not to do! I signed up to go to graduate school! Yes, finally, I was going to get my Master's degree in Systems Engineering. I've always worked full-time while taking university courses, so this would be a piece of cake, right? Wrong.

Now, this time, add the pressures of a more demanding job, living alone, a pandemic, kids doing school at home, and going through a divorce. Regardless, I still finished my degree in 2.5 years, successfully.

See, what I am trying to tell you, is that, we do not owe our life, our success, or our happiness to anyone. No matter what they say or do.

People may facilitate opportunities, but ultimately, you make the choice of taking it and making something great out of it. All you owe that person is a "Thank you." You do not have to stick around if you do not feel valued and appreciated. There are no excuses to accept mistreatment and it is not our job to change an adult to be a better person.

These last two lessons have been reinforced by subsequent people I have met after becoming divorced. We cannot blame others for being unhappy or unsuccessful, these two things come as a result of our choices.

There were two days when I realized what I wanted and they started with a mirror.

The first time, I had just taken a shower and washed my hair at home. I looked at myself in the mirror and absolutely disliked what I saw. I was disgusted at what I had turned into: sad, bitter, loveless, and worn out. I could barely recognize myself. I had no joy in me.

The second time, I was at a hotel room in New York, with a dear lady friend from work, traveling for a work conference. I had showered, did my hair and make-up and looked rested. Nobody was rushing me or waking me up while rudely opening the windows. I was excited to go explore the city with my friend. And, I said to myself: "I wish it could always be like this!" I wanted the feeling of freedom and joy back in my life. And so, I made it happen. It was overdue. It was time to say the words and move out and on before it was too late for me.

Before I knew it, I fell back into my generational trauma pain and fell again into suicidal depression. I fell into suicidal depression a year after I moved out, while divorce negotiation was still going on.

I reached my rock bottom and I didn't know what to do. I was driving and my hands were shaking, I was crying, and all I wanted to do was to drive the car into the ditch as hard as I could. Somehow I made it home and went straight to bed.

My guardian angel worked extra hard that night. The next day I called my friend Elena and we scheduled a call. We spoke once a week for a couple months. At some point, we talked about my pot of yuck. I made a list of all the things that hurt me, that I allowed to happen to me, because I didn't speak out, because I stayed too long in a marriage that almost destroyed me.

All those moments, memories, bad words, feelings were stewing all that time in a simmering pot and I never let them out. I never talked about it. It was rotten. How could I let all that happen?

I needed to forgive myself more than forgiving the man for treating me wrong.

It wasn't until I was able to forgive myself that I felt a huge weight lifted off my shoulders. I could finally breathe. I felt more powerful and full of energy. As I was feeling recharged, I started to consider new challenges. What else could I do? I had a good job, I was working on a Master degree, what else could I do better. I was already working out daily. So, after talking with another friend, she inspired me to train for bodybuilding.

I started training in April and by November of the same year, I took on my first bodybuilding bikini competition. It was scary and exciting all at the same time! This new life I am now in is definitely a challenge of body, mind, and character. I push myself every day to do better in my workouts and improve my eating habits. Not every day is perfect, but it is continuous work towards improvement in all aspects, physical and mental.

The workouts help me release stress, and the hormones produced by the body help me feel better emotionally. I am grateful that I do not have to take medication to help me feel normal. I am a much better person when I workout. A very long walk has the same emotional benefits on rest days. I am very happy with my life right now, I am doing well, and I sleep in as late as I want on the weekends. I am always considering new challenges, travel, and how I can continue to improve my life and my son's life.

Lastly, what I want to tell you is to pay attention to yourself.

Take care of yourself first, so that you can give to others from a full cup, if you are a giving person, like me. You cannot give what you do not have.

Learn to recognize a bad situation. Build up your courage to do the things that are hard, do them afraid, and live your life with joy in your heart. Ask for help when you need it. We can't help if we don't know you need it. I hope my story can inspire you somehow.

Be happy. God bless you.
With love, Rossana

PRAYERS FROM ELENA:

As Rossana shared her story about the courage it took for her to do the "hard things" afraid, she is an inspiration at what the power of mental toughness can do. She recognized change was needed and she had to go through the journey of believing she was worth better, no matter what others may have thought. Can we please take a moment and pray over her, and anyone else who struggles with doubting their worth or questioning their ability to make difficult changes?

Lord Jesus, may you continue to provide your clarity and discernment over Rossana and all those who are in need of courage and bravery to make the changes in their lives necessary so they may be able to experience the joy and fulfillment you intended for them. May you walk alongside them and guide them through each choice and decision they face as they continue to grow and prosper in their abundance of blessings.

In your name…
Amen

CHAPTER 7

MY ROAD TO PEACE

SURRENDER to RISE
R-Resourceful

Chapter written by Jessica Montalvo

Acknowledgements: To my daughter, Lara Juliana Montalvo, who has been the most life changing force of nature that has given my life an entirely new meaning which has connected me to use my voice in ways that I have only dreamed of having the courage to honor. My wish is for you to always understand the beauty in every moment that life shows you and remain resourceful even within the times of chaos.

Early on, I knew I loved making things with my hands. I would use my mother's sewing machine to sew and create things.

My Road to Peace

THE EVOLUTION OF my road to peace has consisted of so many different versions of myself. Some of those versions are so foreign that I don't even recognize who I used to be. I suppose our life experience allows us to go through numerous transformations throughout our journey. Honoring every version of myself has been a very personal road of so many life-altering circumstances with the understanding that nothing is permanent; not even life itself.

If you had asked me five years ago where I would be today, I would have given you a completely different answer than the one I have for you right now in this moment. The many layers of my life can be categorized as bittersweet with more redirection than I would care to acknowledge albeit I still honor and respect. They say that once you're middle aged, it's all downhill from there. But for me, I feel like I'm just getting started.

It has taken me time to unpack the numerous stages of my life that led to the realization and awareness of the abuse, trauma, and pain in which I have endured. Within the layers of my baggage is the inner child I have haphazardly nurtured yet, is a beautiful masterpiece that has taken time to rediscover.

The foundational groundwork I was exposed to showed me just how necessary it was for me to continue being redirected because I lacked the emotional maturity and awareness in which I needed to understand the type of relationships I entertained. There were so many close calls. I was foolish to think that I had any business being where I knew I had no business being.

The exposure to the fighting was the foundational groundwork. The exposure to the many times my mother would run away and eventually come back was the foundational groundwork. The name calling, the yelling, the throwing things, the cursing, even down to that piece of pizza my mother threw at my father telling him out loud for us to hear of her wish for him to choke on it and die. It was that foundational groundwork that became a broken record. I mean, how could I understand the dynamic of toxic behavior when there was no explanation. And how could I know that it had nothing to do with me until so many years later of truly understanding what abuse is.

You don't understand the influence it has on your life until you do.

I have never felt completely connected to my parents. I tried so many times to have something in common with them other than my name. I so desperately wanted to feel a part of something, sometimes. I believe it was this significant lack of emotional connection that led me to discovering the various elements of each of them in other people, which led me down paths I should not have taken.

There was a glimpse of me in there, somewhere. That innate knowing that I didn't quite fit in, didn't know my place in the world, but knew it was not the one assigned to me.

Almost All Out of Faith

The people I have met along the way have made me believe in every part of myself. I escaped with my life intact but rewired. Mental health and mental illness education had become a life theme of my trying to make sense of men who embodied peculiar elements of what I later realized were elements of my father. Narcissistic abuse is detrimental to anyone, and potentially deadly for those who do not know any other behavior to compare it to.

I lost my short-term memory because of such mental abuse. My first ex-husband was in the military, as was my father. My spirit deteriorated enough for me to lose my ability to walk, having to have back surgery and relearn how to walk. I would later find out that he was bipolar and suffered from PTSD after he became suicidal and homicidal, and I was in fear for my life.

The next relationship I had was with a covert narcissist. When my spirit was deteriorating due to his narcissistic abuse and his addictions, my back took me down a second time. He was so angry that I required care. In fact, on the very day of my scheduled spinal injection, he cut off the service to my phone so I couldn't call anyone to take me to my procedure. And after the divorce was finalized, he harassed me.

As if these two didn't do it for me, the third time was most definitely the charm. For me, it was the ultimate betrayal.

When I discovered that the very person I thought I would be building a foundation with turned out to be like the others that have come before him, I was absolutely devastated. I had never seen the two lines before, distinct, and obvious, in the traditional bubble gum pink color in all their two lined glory. I would learn about what it was like to be on my pregnancy journey all alone. There is no child support. There is no contact. There is, however, the most amazing girl that I have ever had the privilege to love. And I will protect her with every fiber of my being, rebuilding a life that is truly meant for us.

I was almost all out of faith until I truly understood that they made me believe in every part of myself.

The Art of Letting Go

There is an art to letting go. It's allowing what is, to be.

Coming to terms with the fact that there is nothing traditional about my life has been quite the process of reconciliation both emotionally and mentally. I don't think that any part of my life will ever be traditional, either. I no longer find myself feeling inadequate when I explain to my daughter that some families have just one mommy and one daughter. I saw the destruction of a so-called traditional family unit in my own upbringing and made peace with it. I knew that I owed my daughter and our little family a real foundation. I feel like I've been given a second chance at life with God continuing to protect us.

Find Your Passion and You'll Find Your Voice

Despite the foundational groundwork and the varying unsustainable circumstances along the way, there have always been glimpses of peace throughout my journey. Early on, I knew I loved making things with my hands. I would use my mother's sewing machine to sew and create things. It was a skill she taught me that I embraced because it was a connection that was unique to me and her.

As I developed my spark for creativity, my artistic expressions became collections of notebooks of drafts of sketches and drawings with some added color from either crayons or colored pencils. I would even make fashionable clothing and accessories and would design and sew them for my Barbie's. I would label the types of fabric I would dream of using, and how I would want each item to look. And through these waves of inspiration, I would teach myself how to make clothes and how to draw with oil pastels and chalk. I didn't know it at the time, but I would even design my business logo in 2011, a year before I even began my business. It would take me twelve years to launch my business as an LLC and rebrand with my own original artwork as the face of Flairware Boutique.

Flairware Boutique started as a hobby. At the time, I was exploring the world of pinup girl style and the iconic silhouettes from the 1950's, making my best attempt to learn how to embrace my femininity. I grew up watching Ginger Rogers and Fred Astaire sweeping the floor with such elegance and always noted the flowy gowns and gorgeous lines of the wiggle dresses, wishing I had my own pretty dresses to wear. I think that's why I own so many of them.

I took pride in wearing my dresses and took an interest in owning accessories from the 1950's to complement my evolving pinup style. I became passionate about looking for antique shops that housed vintage gloves, hats, and scarves and I would soon become immersed with learning how to make my own hair flowers, bows, and other accessories that would pay homage to the classic and timeless vintage style with a modern twist of new materials that would withstand constant wear.

For every dress I owned, I made unique accessories to go with them. It was then that I decided to embrace my passion and empower myself to offer handmade items to anyone who appreciated the products I became so passionate about making. I soon would be sending my products all over the Midwest, sponsoring pinup contests, non-profit organizations, silent auctions, and ladies who identified with the style.

Makeup wasn't too far away. As I learned about the fashion, I also learned about the makeup and hairstyles to enhance and complete an entire look.

The Evolution of The Pinup Girl

I have not always been confident; I never had any reason to be. I think as a woman, it's easy to understand why we battle with our physical appearances. We learn at a young age that we are judged by the way we look with constant media shoving fads and diets down our throats. Not to mention, some men, especially in certain cultures, have a way with making women feel uncomfortable because of how they've been conditioned to see us as objects. From being stalked, to catcalls and actual barking, I have experienced times where I have felt uneasy being a woman. Try also having a mother who constantly discouraged any glimmer of self-esteem when being called fat was a regular occurrence because of her own misery. I was on my way to receive my master's degree, for example, and although I was in the best shape of my life at that time, her comment reminded me that if I were to lose more weight, I would look better in my dress. These things stay with you as you navigate your identity. I believe it is why I embraced my own evolution as a pinup girl.

Understanding the importance of finding myself within the rubble, it was the connection to the style that brought me back to who I am.

Start Over as Many Times as You Need

The question I have recently asked myself is, can we become our inner child again even after all we have experienced? Start over as many times as you need to answer this question with a yes.

People come and go to and from our lives like the tide. Some are meant to stay for a couple of chapters in our book of life and some are meant for just one. No matter what it looks like, it is to be embraced for what it becomes, how it evolves, and then released when and if the time comes to release it. Sometimes all we are meant to experience is just a chapter. And what makes it beautiful is the memories and lessons it leaves behind.

The idea is to understand that what others think doesn't matter. No one lives our life. We live our life. And when someone judges our decisions, that is none of our business. Life is not a one size fits all approach. It is not our place to decide other people's life choices for them. We all have our own to create.

Start where you are. You don't have to have everything figured out.

Healing from this journey has been a most magnificent adventure. I realized through time, that every regret my parents ever had was projected onto their children. And it was as if I was trying to make them proud of me in search of praise that I would never receive, and if I did, I didn't truly believe it. I did what I was told. I pursued the degrees they wanted me to pursue. I denied certain parts of me that wanted to be alive. And in the process of trying to figure out who I was, I lost myself several times. My silent vow to be an example for others was crucial to the commitment I made to myself that I wouldn't be like them; even though so many aspects of my life I had failed miserably to live up to. But the awareness I have today has allowed me to truly be present with the best version of myself.

I take pride in being a comeback queen. Like I said, I'm just getting started.

PRAYERS FROM ELENA:

As Jessica shared her story about becoming the person she was meant to be all along, and using her gifts right in front of her, to tap into her inner child so that she may become the woman God intended, we are reminded of the power of our youth.

Lord Jesus, may you always bring laughter, joy, and genuine peace into Jessica's life and may you cover her daughter in your protective arms so that she may always know the beauty of the love you so freely give. May all those who find it hard to remember the playfulness that life is meant to carry, be reminded that we can enjoy this journey, even through our trials.

In your name...

Amen

CHAPTER 8

BELIEVE IN YOURSELF

SURRENDER to RISE
E-Envision

Chapter written by Melinda Heller

Acknowledgements: To Richard Heller and Natalie Smith for always believing and supporting me.

There were several bumps in the road, but I got it done.

THERE IS NOTHING more terrifying than looking into the future and not seeing much of anything special.

I mean, everyone's always talking about making all these great plans for the future, right, so why was it that I couldn't see anything when I looked into mine? It was like I was staring at a blank screen, wondering when the hope, joy, love, laughter, and excitement would appear.

I began wondering, How did I get here? How did I get to this place where I could no longer recognize my life? How did I become this woman that continued moving about, day after day, looking like she had it all together, when in fact, inside I was really carrying this heavy feeling of alienation. It's like I had become an outcast looking in on this fantastic shell of a life and all I could feel was the void and emptiness it carried.

Have you ever felt the fear that strikes when you look into the future and can't see much of anything special? It can be terrifying.

I began telling myself that I needed to get to know God better. I felt, from somewhere deep within, that God was the missing piece in my life. But how? How do you begin to get to know God better?

It's funny that the moment I began asking myself this question, God answered. He answered by giving me an opportunity to go on a "spiritual girl's trip" with a dear friend.

Trust me, I needed convincing to go and I'm so glad my friend didn't give up on me as she literally had to talk me into going.

As I prepared for this trip, I began asking myself, what was it that I really wanted God to reveal to me.

Well, let me tell you Sister, I was not expecting all that God placed right in front of me. It became clear that there were things I had to face and push through, so that I could actually begin to envision what was ahead.

I share this with you, just in case you ever find yourself not being able to see anything happy and bright ahead of you. It's there, trust me, keep looking and listening.

I found myself taken back to my mom. What? Yes, my mom, to when she had cancer. But it was more than that, it was a time in my life when I knew my marriage was over but I didn't have the strength to even look at that part of my life, all I could see was my mom, and her cancer.

I felt horrible because I knew divorce was inevitable, but I didn't want to even start that process until my mom passed away. I felt horrible for even thinking about it that way. Like who was I to take something so traumatic and choose to make it convenient.

Layers of guilt started to bury how I was really feeling about it all.

As time passed, I did get through my divorce, but not without believing most of it was "my fault" and to be honest, I think a lot of women think this. Of course, it takes two people to make a marriage work, so why do women carry the solo burden of thinking it's their fault when a marriage falls apart?

As I spent time on my spiritual getaway, which really became my spiritual renewal, I reflected on many things that I had brushed under the rug and just stepped around, but God said I couldn't do that any more.

I had to face things my husband had hid from me for so many years. Funny thing is, as he shared information that he had held inside for years, I had to wonder what was I to do with this information now? I mean, he told me so that he could release the burden and guilt he was carrying, and so that he could clear his own mind, but what was I supposed to do with this bomb of information now heavy on my own heart.

As I tried to talk about it with my family, and sort through my own emotions, it became even more confusing to learn that many of my family weren't even surprised by what I was sharing.

How is it they weren't shocked, but I was? Talk about a state of self-doubt, low self-worth, and even a feeling of lack of trust in my own self-judgment. It's like there was a feeling of betrayal on many levels.

As I sorted all of this out during the spiritual trip, I understood it all had purpose. I understood none of this was by accident and it could make me a better person if I allowed it to.

As I started living my life again, and getting back to a new normal, I found myself smiling again. I also found myself married to a wonderful man who was a huge support to me in every aspect of my life.

There are times when it seems as one thing calms down another one stirs up.

As things were going great in my marriage, and I was being treated with love, respect, and support, I realized how much was being taken from me, and for granted, at my job. I could now recognize how under appreciated I had been and I now had the self confidence to know I deserved better.

I remember when I got home from my spiritual trip, I told my husband how I was feeling, and I shared with him how I felt God was letting me know it was time to leave my job even though I didn't quite know what was next. There wasn't a plan beyond me leaving but my husband said it was time and encouraged my resignation. That's as far as I could see, and after being there for 11 years, I, once again, was walking into the unknown.

Only this time, I knew it was different. I knew God was with me because I had taken the time to strengthen my relationship with Him.

This was another point of surrender for me. I never realized there could be so many points of surrender in the journey we call life, but here I was, once again, trying to envision a new life with another new start and praying, and I mean praying hard, while I surrendered to God's will for me.

It's taken me a lot to understand that there is incredible strength in the moment of surrender. You must believe you are worthy of better than where you are now. You must focus on the blessing you have rather than look at the fear that could be waiting for you around the corner. You have to believe the life you envision is within reach and focus on doing what it takes to make it come into focus.

All I knew is I wanted to be joyful, and happy, and truly know I was a child of God and a woman of God that was blessed with gifts to share with the world and I was not here only to be stepped on and looked over by everyone that crossed my path. I was here because I made a difference.

Today, I am so much lighter and I do live with joy. I can envision a future full of love with my husband, and with the work I now do, and I am proud of the impact I make.

Believing in yourself is not always the easiest thing in the world to do, but it's the most rewarding journey to embark on. Take some time to get to know your God, and watch how beautiful your world truly becomes. Trust me, it's better than you could ever envision for yourself.

PRAYERS FROM ELENA:

As Melinda shared many examples of what it truly means to wipe the slate clean and start from scratch, it is a reminder that there is always a vision from God even when we can't see it. She is a true representation of what it means to begin to walk in faith and how beautiful the journey can be.

Lord Jesus, may you continue to guide Melinda and all those who follow you, especially on the days when they feel lost. May you always remain the compass that leads us straight into fulfillment and purpose. May you be a constant reminder that even in the moments of unknown, we are not lost and we need to simply keep our eyes on You.

In your name...
Amen

CHAPTER 9

BRAVE WOMAN

SURRENDER to RISE
N-Navigate

Chapter written by Brittany Buesching

Acknowledgements: Little did I comprehend the profound significance of those who played a pivotal role in the trials of my life, for they have become the very bedrock of my strength today. While you may perceive only a single facet of their being, it is imperative to acknowledge the duality that resides within each of us–a delicate interplay of light and shadow. In this moment of gratitude, I wholeheartedly express my appreciation for the brighter aspects of those individuals who have graced my narrative, my father, my mother, my ex-boyfriend, my grandmother, and my grandmother's former husband. Despite the challenges we faced together, it is vital to recognize that my love and care for them endure unwaveringly. Rather, it is in the crucible of those trials and the wisdom I gleaned from them that I have embarked upon a path leading to a life brimming with genuine happiness and fulfillment.

...and the bravery required to navigate the challenging terrain of my own life.

IMAGINE A YOUNG woman caught in an enduring struggle with fear, neglect, abandonment, and an overwhelming sense of worthlessness. That young woman was me, navigating the challenging waters of my childhood. The painful aftermath of my parents' divorce left me feeling like a soul adrift, constantly shifting between homes amidst bitter custody battles. I questioned every decision, burdened by the belief that I was responsible for the broken love that once united my family.

But let me share the truth—I was merely a child, pure and yearning for the love and stability that constantly eluded me, slipping away like grains of sand. No one could have foreseen the immense pain that gripped my heart, suffocating me in a sea of neglect and abandonment. I witnessed my father remarry multiple times, his attention shifting away from his own children. Meanwhile, my mother descended into the depths of substance abuse, her presence in our lives becoming sporadic, leaving me with an intense longing for the motherly bond I desperately desired.

Among my siblings, I carried the burden of the most profound wounds. I was the middle child, grappling with self-doubt and academic challenges. Hurtful taunts, such as "Lear queer," echoed in my mind, leaving invisible marks on my vulnerable soul. My father, preoccupied with his new partners and engrossed in work, remained unaware of the tears I cried in solitude. Meanwhile, my mother drifted in and out of our lives, creating an emptiness in my heart that felt insurmountable to overcome.

In the midst of my despair, I yearned to break free from a life that made me feel insignificant. I experienced bullying, abandonment, and emotional exhaustion, holding onto the notion that my presence held no meaning. Even at a tender age, the heaviness of my anguish led me to contemplate ending my life. The thought that nobody would notice my absence overwhelmed me, enveloping my fragile heart in a stifling web.

Yet, what intensified these feelings of despair was the presence of my stepmother during my father's second-to-last marriage. At the delicate age of 11, I found myself caught in a distressing nightmare, enduring torment that no child should ever face. She distorted my perception of reality, tainting my breakfast with motor oil and chasing me through the house with a knife, leaving me trembling with fear. Once again, I was overwhelmed by an overwhelming sense of inadequacy. Summoning my courage, I confided in my father, hoping to find refuge in his protection, but he disregarded my pleas for assistance, turning a blind eye to my suffering.

So, I made a choice—the most courageous choice I could muster at the young age of 11. I ran away, finding myself labeled as a troubled youth in a world that had failed to shield me. It might not have been the wisest decision, but in that moment of desperation, I had to take charge of my own destiny. The world took notice, though not all of the attention was positive. I encountered hostility from my stepmother, anger from my father, and even the disapproval of the legal system. Yet, amidst the depths of my turmoil, I held onto a flicker of understanding—I sensed deep within my soul that I possessed a purpose, a life worth fighting for.

Amidst the tears and the scars, I maintained the faith that a better future awaited me, an upcoming chapter filled with brightness and hope. This belief served as my driving force, even when the burdens of life seemed unbearable. Confronting challenges head-on, I unearthed the resilient power within the human spirit—the capacity to transcend the shadows and embrace the radiance of life.

As you read my story, I hope you discover comfort in the truth that even during our darkest moments, there is a purpose to our being. We may encounter stumbling blocks and setbacks, yet deep inside us lies a strength that can withstand any tempest. May you gather the bravery to navigate your own challenges, to pursue the brighter chapters that lie ahead, and to understand that your life holds immeasurable value, deserving of resilience and perseverance.

I bore the weighty burden of feeling undeserving, forsaken, and overlooked by those who were meant to offer love and guidance. The imprints of childhood wounds left lasting marks on my spirit, casting a lingering shade over my adult life. In moments of deep despair, I often pondered how I had withstood such anguish without yielding to the overpowering urge to escape my own existence.

During my teenage years, I reached a critical juncture. Overwhelmed by despair, I ventured into the realm of oblivion, seeking solace in the prospect of eternal rest. In that pivotal instant, I ingested numerous Tylenol PM pills, clinging to the belief that peaceful sleep would grant me relief from the torment that consumed me. However, instead of encountering empathy and understanding, I faced reproachful words and accusations of selfishness.

My Family claimed I was surrounded by an abundance of love, implying that I had no justification for harboring such somber thoughts. Superficially, their statement held some truth. However, those words penetrated my wounded heart and reverberated through my fractured mind. In moments of profound isolation, I contemplated the gravity of their accusations, all while longing for the refuge of authentic love and acceptance.

But here's the irony—the individuals who would genuinely love and cherish me had yet to cross my path. Those words, uttered in a moment of misunderstanding, lingered in the depths of my consciousness. They acted as a persistent reminder of the courage I needed to summon, and the bravery required to navigate the challenging terrain of my own life.

Can you discern the recurring thread that weaves through the fabric of my journey? It is the unwavering call to be courageous, to transcend the pain and shadows that threatened to engulf my spirit. Through each trial I faced, I discovered that bravery was not merely a choice; it became my lifeline—an anchor that kept me steadfast amidst the tempestuous seas of my existence.

And so, I embraced the recurring theme, allowing it to shape and mold me into a resilient warrior. I learned to draw strength from vulnerability and to seek healing in the face of adversity. While the scars of my past remain, they stand as a testament to the battles I fought and continue to wage.

In the symphony of my life, the recurring melody of bravery plays on, propelling me forward with unwavering persistence. Through the courage to confront my darkest moments, I have discovered the limitless capacity of the human spirit to heal, to grow, and ultimately to find solace in the embrace of self-love.

During a time of darkness, I was once again enveloped by unspeakable pain and torment. The echoes of mental abuse reverberated within my mind, serving as a constant reminder of my vulnerability. In the midst of a nightmare, I endured an unimaginable violation—an assault on my body that left me shattered and scarred.

Through these harrowing trials, I confronted the true essence of strength and bravery. The flames of adversity threatened to engulf me, but I refused to let them extinguish the flicker of resilience burning within. However, as I battled my own demons, I uncovered another agonizing truth—one that pierced my heart with searing pain. My beloved grandmother, the pillar of strength in my life, found herself trapped in an abusive relationship with her own husband.

The weight of this revelation crashed upon me like a tidal wave, leaving me gasping for air. How could I face my own trauma while witnessing the suffering of someone so dear to me? Summoning every ounce of courage, I confided in my grandmother, sharing the burden of my own abuse. In that shared vulnerability, we embarked on a treacherous legal journey together, navigating the daunting obstacles that lay ahead.

Our intertwined experiences taught us the enduring strength of resilience and forgiveness. Side by side, we fought for justice, unwavering in our determination to break free from the chains that bound us. Yet, in my unwavering pursuit of bravery, I unintentionally overlooked other vital virtues—forgiveness and compassion. The pain that had haunted me since childhood clung tightly to my soul, stifling my capacity to release and move on.

Fear, like a constant companion, fueled my courage, but it left little room for forgiveness or compassion to flourish.

It wasn't until my adult years, on the cusp of self-discovery, that I began to embrace the transformative power of compassion and the art of letting go. It proved to be a tender journey, a path marked by tears shed for the wounds of the past. However, through the fractures in my broken heart, love and forgiveness began to bloom.

Now, as I reflect upon the challenging terrain I traversed, I carry the weight of my experiences as a testament to the resilience of the human spirit. Life's journey weaves together threads of both joy and pain, resilience and vulnerability. And amidst my own struggles, I discovered that by embracing compassion and releasing the burdens of the past, true healing can take root.

Fast forward to my later teenage years, after graduating from high school, I felt a longing in my heart for something more, something that would whisk me away from the stagnant life I had known. It was during this time that I stumbled upon a program that offered the opportunity to become a flight attendant—a glimmer of hope in a world that had grown dull and predictable. The mere thought of soaring through the clouds, leaving behind the familiar streets and faces that had become tiresome, ignited a fire within me. It was a chance to escape the confines of my hometown, a place that no longer felt like home.

As I immersed myself in the demanding training, I held onto the belief that this journey would be my path to self-discovery. The possibility of unraveling the mysteries of the world and connecting with diverse souls who could reshape my perspective fueled my determination. I yearned to break free from the grip of despair that threatened to engulf me.

Yet, amidst the excitement and anticipation, there was a shadow—a toxic and abusive relationship that had ensnared me. In my naivety, I mistook the manipulative torment for genuine love, driven by the desperate desire to fill the void inside me. It bound my spirit and cast a dark cloud over my dreams, threatening to extinguish the flicker of hope I had carefully nurtured.

However, even in the midst of suffocating darkness, a glimmer of resilience remained. Each day, I fought to reclaim my agency, to break free from the suffocating grasp of that destructive bond. It was a battle fought within my heart, a struggle against self-doubt and fear. And in that battle, I learned that sometimes, the most challenging obstacles we face lie within ourselves.

Slowly but steadily, I began to untangle the threads of manipulation, piecing together fragments of my shattered self-esteem. It was a painful process, a journey of self-reflection and healing that demanded every ounce of strength I possessed. But as I emerged from the shadows, I realized that true love does not reside in control and anguish. It flourishes in kindness, respect, and genuine compassion.

Now, as I reflect on that tumultuous chapter of my life, gratitude fills my heart. Gratitude for the trials that tested my resilience, for the scars that bear witness to my strength. The journey to becoming a flight attendant was not just a physical one—it was a transformative odyssey that liberated my spirit and taught me the immeasurable value of self-love.

In the end, I discovered that sometimes, the most profound journey we embark on is the one that leads us back home—to ourselves.

Now, I find myself at the threshold of a new phase in my life, reflecting on the turbulent relationship that consumed me. In that dark place, hurtful words pierced my vulnerable heart like daggers. I was called names that shattered my self-worth—labels I believed from a man who claimed to love me. I held onto that toxic relationship for far too long, allowing those venomous words to poison my spirit.

However, as I stepped away from the flight industry, I realized that my purpose had yet to fully reveal itself. I had no clear vision of what it should be or how it should manifest. Serendipitously, my sister and I made the decision together to join the army. Little did I know that this new chapter would become a mental battleground of its own. Courage became the foundation of everything I was called to do and embody. It demanded that I summon the strength within to confront my fears head-on.

Once again, I found myself leaving behind a toxic relationship, recognizing the need to nurture my own strength and discover my true purpose. This journey required more time away, more moments of self-discovery. And you know what? It was exactly what I needed to cultivate resilience.

In the face of adversity, I learned that I was capable of far more than I had ever imagined. The scars of emotional abuse began to heal as I embraced my own worth and potential. I realized that my parents' limitations did not define me. I made a vow to prove the naysayers wrong and rise above the labels that haunted me for far too long.

As I stand here now, I want you to know that the journey to self-discovery and empowerment is not always smooth. It is a challenging path, filled with obstacles and moments of doubt. Yet, within each of us lies the strength to endure, the resilience to overcome, and the capacity to embrace our true purpose.

May my story serve as a reminder that you, too, possess the power to break free from toxic relationships, to find your own strength, and to uncover a purpose that ignites your soul. Embrace the journey, for it is through the challenges that we discover our true selves.

The army undeniably played a vital role in nurturing my bravery and empowering me to break free from the toxic relationship that held me captive. It was a defining moment, etched into the core of my being, when he dared to lay his hands on me, attempting to suffocate my spirit. In that terrifying instant, my military training became my shield, and my instincts became my guiding light.

Summoning every ounce of courage within, I took control of the situation, refusing to be a victim any longer. I fought back, defending myself against his oppressive grip. And in the chaos of that moment, I delivered a blow I never thought I would, a physical manifestation of the strength I had discovered within.

It was a painful realization, understanding that I had to cause harm to protect myself from the domestic turmoil he had inflicted upon me. Yet, in that act of self-defense, I found a newfound sense of empowerment, a testament to the resilience growing within me. The chains that had bound me for far too long shattered, replaced by a fierce determination to reclaim my independence and pave a path of healing and self-discovery.

As you read my words, I hope you can sense the raw intensity of that moment. It was a turning point, an instant that forever altered the course of my life. The army had instilled in me the courage to stand tall, to fight for my well-being, and to refuse to be silenced or controlled.

May my story serve as a reminder that each of us possesses a wellspring of strength waiting to be tapped into. We have the power to break free from toxic relationships, reclaim our independence, and build a future defined by love, self-respect, and unwavering determination. Embrace your own bravery, for it is through the darkest moments that we discover the limitless potential within ourselves.

Now, honestly, I didn't have to share all of this history. But what I want to convey is that no matter how deep life plunges or how much you struggle, there are certain values that must be nurtured to truly embrace your best self: courage, fear, compassion, forgiveness, and commitment. Fear is inevitable, but courage is the foundation for conquering it. Being brave is the most extraordinary superpower one can possess.

As I reflect on my current situation, I admit that I feel fear. Running a business can be daunting. However, I draw courage from every woman I work with at Bravely You boudoir. They not only leave my business feeling confident, but they also find the strength to love themselves again, without relying on anyone else. While it's wonderful to receive love from others, true love must come from within.

My name is Brittany Buesching, and I am the proud owner of Bravely You boudoir, a photography business dedicated to empowering women and celebrating their bodies. We help women find strength in their personal history, overcome their struggles, and heal the wounds that have affected their self-worth. Our goal is to instill in them 100% confidence, self-love, and respect.

While it's important to live for others, we mustn't forget to live for ourselves. If you constantly find yourself on your knees, living solely for someone else, how can you find true love and fulfillment? You are no longer a child burdened by the past. Let go of that history, release it, forgive it boldly. Move forward with bravery, allowing courage to shape your future steps.

Let the power of courage guide you as you embark on this journey of self-discovery, self-acceptance, and self-love.

PRAYERS FROM ELENA:

As Brittany has mastered the art of showing bravery through vulnerability she encompasses the essence of pure strength amongst beauty. The gift she has been given to capture the light that shines from within each of us, makes her one of the brightest lights to be around. Her spirit is steadfast and she's someone you feel better for knowing.

Lord Jesus, may you continue to cover Brittany and her beautiful family in your love and grace. May you always be a constant reminder that there is light at all times and in all things. Continue to bless her with the ability to do your work as she helps others through the lens of love and bravery, making this world a more beautiful place.

In your name...
Amen

CHAPTER 10

I AM NOT A STATISTIC

SURRENDER to RISE
D-Discipline

Chapter written by Dawn Rodriguez

Acknowledgements: I'd like to thank all of the strong women in my life who have helped mold me into the woman I am today and to God for giving me the love to grow through it all.

We are not statistics, life happens, we are not who the world says we are. We have the power to change our course of life. All we need is the will and the guts to do it.

NO ONE GIVES you an instruction manual on life. No one can prepare you for the things that are about to happen or even things you have no idea could possibly happen. Some may try to warn you as you grow up, but do you really ever listen? Or do you just have to learn things the hard way? Sometimes that's the only choice some of us have.

That's where I found myself over and over again growing up, always having to find things out the hard way. At times it was something I laughed about since I usually found a way out of it, but when you're not the only one on the hot mess express, that's when life gets sticky.

When you're a teen mom having to raise a child on your own while dad sits in prison, there are no more laughs.

There comes a moment when you are left sitting there wondering how you ruined your whole life and you can't ask anyone because they aren't there to help you, they're only there to remind you what a piece of crap statistic you are, that's where I was.

I was alone and knew I had messed up, and instead of people being there for me, the people who meant the world to me, it was like the world was there just to remind me I was nothing. Only thing is, the world didn't realize the fire I had blazing in me and I was determined to prove everyone wrong one day. I would show them I was something.

I can still remember when I found out the news of the beautiful life growing inside me. I was 16 yrs old, living the fast life and in love with a gang-banger. It was hard to believe at first, but I was somehow not as upset as you would imagine a teen mom in my situation would be.

Actually, a part of me secretly felt happy thinking somehow, this baby would bring us closer and he'd never ever leave me. Funny right? I think the need to keep people from leaving stemmed from my childhood.

With an absent father, negligent mother and stepfather who physically and sexually abused me since I was 6 yrs old, it was hard to believe I was worth loving and sticking around for. I was sure this baby would change all of that. My silly ass had no idea the reality check that was about to unfold.

My family suggested I give the baby up for adoption because, "what would the neighbors think." My boyfriend's family, on the other hand, was thrilled. Coming from a long line of poverty, this was normal for them. I had so much reassurance from his sister that I could have Medicaid, Foodstamps, WIC and welfare help me out so life was actually going to be pretty amazing! I mean, all I had to do was keep having babies so I could get more money from the government, yay!!

I didn't worry much because I was sure my boyfriend and I would stick together, figure our life out and face all of our problems head on. That was until he decided to commit a crime that would land him in prison for many years and land me as a single teen mom trying to figure life out on my own.

As a high school drop out, I realized my options for the future were slim and that I needed to go back to school so my baby and I didn't fall through the cracks of poverty forever. Only problem was the school didn't want me back because of all the trouble I caused while I was there. Plus, I was already 18 yrs old with a baby by this time so they suggested I obtain my GED instead.

Expectations for me were low since I decided to ruin my life I guess.

As the years went on, I was able to finally get that high school diploma, find a job and make a nice little life for my son and I. Even though we didn't have furniture and used empty boxes as our dinner table, we were still happy. If I had kept my head on straight, this is the part where things would be looking up, but coming from a childhood of chaos, I couldn't let things be that easy. I mean, I was still young; I still had so many more poor life decisions to make! Depression and the need for love would take over and I would eventually go back to drugs and alcohol to numb my thoughts.

The party life was so fulfilling. Alcohol for me to forget, drugs to make me feel good and men to fill the hole in my heart.

I thought that as long as I was there to put my son to bed at night with a bedtime story, get him to school on time and cook dinner for us, I was doing my part as a mom. After all, what else are mothers good for? It wasn't until the day I almost lost my life to this self destruction that I realized I wasn't going to live long enough to see my son grow up. I was all he had. I wasn't ready to go, who was going to take care of him? No one was going to love him as much as I did.

It suddenly dawned on me that I had become the piece of crap statistic the world said I would be. Just another Latina teen mom from the hood, roaming the streets, addicted to drugs and alcohol, doing nothing with her life... After 6 yrs of wasting away my life and self worth, I decided there had to be a change. I decided I had to reignite that fire inside of me that pushed me to fulfill a higher destiny. I decided to do what no one else expected me to do. I decided to do the one thing that I could do to guarantee a secure life for my son's future. I decided to go back to school.

I figured going into the field of nursing would be my best bet. since nurses get paid pretty decently and they never seem to be out of a job. As I made my way back to school, registering for my classes and feeling so overjoyed that our lives were about to change for the better, I realized I was pregnant again, this time with a little girl. Knowing that this journey was going to be even more difficult, I was eagerly determined to see it through. Now I had two lives to be responsible for, there was no more time to waste. No one else was going to pull us out into a better life. It was all up to me.

I knew I had to teach myself methods of discipline and time management to make this work. The new baby's dad being the immature and inconsiderate person he was would blast the TV so loud, it was hard to study. I often found myself on the bathroom floor, with earplugs on and study guides scattered across the floor as my study space. I was pregnant with a huge belly at this time, so I threw some pillows in there too. I continued to work while attending school. I hated the predicament I put myself in, but I was determined not to give up.

As the years passed and I made my way through school, I noticed my surroundings were no longer the same. My friends I used to party with were no longer there. I missed weddings, funerals, birthday parties, Mothers day and all kinds of special occasions so that I could have more time to study. I wouldn't allow anything or anyone to stop me or get in the way.

While I was in Nursing school, some of the students were single moms, some were going through divorces, some had recently lost a family member and some of the students got pregnant during their time there. What I found was that I was among a badass tribe of unstoppable women and men unwilling to allow life circumstances stand between them and their dreams. These were definitely my people.

I continued along, throughout grad school and finally finished with a Masters degree certifying me to become a Family Nurse Practitioner. (show excitement) I had my two children beside me at the end of it all. They watched me struggle, cry and fight to make my dreams come true. Best of all, I had finally put myself in a position to take care of my family without anyone's help. I could support us as a single mom and not have to worry about putting up with anyone's crap along the way. To think of my journey and how it all started (maybe shorten) as an abused child, followed by a teen mom, followed by persistent poor life choices, only to end up here brought me to tears.

I never would've thought I would be where I am today. My purpose in life is to reach out to other young girls and women who are going through struggles to let them know they can turn it all around and pull themselves out of the rut. We are not statistics, life happens, we are not who the world says we are. We have the power to change our course of life. All we need is the will and the guts to do it.

*Where did the guidance come from, what let me here. Grandma, Aunt Liz

PRAYERS FROM ELENA:

As Dawn shared what it really means to defeat the odds and break the cycles of negativity that can be passed down through the generations, she is a true warrior and has a spirit that cannot be stopped. She is an inspiration to many who feel there is no way out and shows others what determination and discipline can do in life.

Lord Jesus, may you continue to bless Dawn and her family with your strength. May you allow her a safe space to be vulnerable with you as she refuels daily with your love and wisdom. May you give her the guidance to lead by example as others look upon her for inspiration and hope. May you bring love, light, laughter, joy, and rest to her with each day.

In your name...
Amen

CHAPTER 11

DO WHAT MAKES YOU ROLL

SURRENDER to RISE
E-Execute

Chapter written by Elena Rodriguez

Acknowledgements: To my parents who gave me a warrior's spirit that cannot be tamed and knows no other way but to love fiercely. Thank you.

Healing is the foundation dreams are built upon.–
Elena Rodriguez

RIP OFF THE band-aid Baby Girl. It's time to let that wound be exposed so it can begin to heal.

When I was going through my divorce with my first husband, I beat myself up for being so "simple". I wondered what was wrong with me that I didn't need all the fluff, the long explanations, the creative story fillers, or even the excuses.

I just wanted to know what was happening, what I needed to do, and to get on with things so I could figure out what was next for me and my boys.

My dad began calling me everyday when he found out I was going through a divorce, and one night he happened to leave me a message saying "Elena, you are not simple. You are honest. There's a difference…" The message went on to say "Do what makes you roll."

That's been a recurring theme in my life, *Do what makes you roll*, but I can't say I always did.

Many people that know me today, always want to know how I "came back" from discovering an affair after my husband died. (That was husband #2 by the way) and I share that story a lot. I don't hide from it and I carry no shame in it, and I share it as a reminder that, you too, can come back strong even after every ounce of confidence has been stripped from you.

But how did I get there? Like, how did I get with a man that could do that to me? What role did I play in it?

See, I'm a little bit different because I don't think it's everyone else's fault. I don't believe I had nothing to do with having my own heart ripped to shreds. I chose my partner. I chose the relationship. I stepped into the cage and chose to watch the key turn and lock me in, but why?

I can't remember how old I was when I learned this other saying "You do what you gotta do." But I do know I was about 8 or 9 years old when I told it to my dad, as I helped him load up his trunk with belongings so he could move across the country to marry someone else and carry on happily ever after with his new family.

You do what you gotta do...what does an 8 year old know about that? Nothing really, but somehow, I just wanted to make sure everyone else felt better about the hot mess our lives were in and I didn't want anyone to have to worry about me.

I didn't want to cause any more stress, drama, problems, so I was always "OK"...but was I really?

The funny thing about "Go Mode" which is where I live most days today, and the place that allows me to accomplish much and build my dream, is that it serves you best only when you've taken the time to heal the things that have hurt you.

Otherwise, Go Mode is just an opportunity to hide from yourself.

When God allowed me to discover my husband's affair, 9 months after I buried him, I broke. That was truly my crumbling point, but I immediately started looking for the gifts in the discovery.

You see, I was grateful to God that He allowed me time before discovering it. If I had learned of the affair, at the same time I learned I had no money, no retirement, no property, no home, I don't think I would have survived.

Instead, I looked at the gift as God laying it all down gently for me. One piece at a time, He placed all this discovery before me and it came in the order that He knew I would be able to work through it, piece by piece, and process it all.

You see, when someone cheats in a relationship it says more about them, than it does about you. Trust me, if someone wants to cheat, they are going to cheat, no matter what you do. It's not about you.

What I realized though, is I am pretty sure I saw the signs of this affair taking place even while we were together, so was I really shocked? Was I really surprised? Or had I just been in denial for far too long.

I almost began to feel a sense of relief after discovering his affair because it made things make sense. Does that make sense?

Like, all the times I was made to believe I was crazy in my head for asking questions, I really wasn't. All the times I felt that icky feeling in my gut and knew something was off, I wasn't imagining it. All the times I would walk on eggshells because I never knew when the mood was going to switch and he would go off on me, I wasn't paranoid. It all made sense. I began to give myself permission to feel the feels and I started to be kind to myself.

I started asking myself, why did I choose to stay and why did I always try harder to do better, be better, forgive more, to make him happy? Why was his happiness more important than my own?

Here was my band-aid moment, and here's what I found when I ripped it off…I was afraid to be left alone again. Ouch!

You see, for all of my life I held on to the belief that if my own dad could leave me, the man that is supposed to look at me and see the most beautiful baby girl in the whole wide world, the man that is supposed to love me first and most… could leave me, hell, any man could leave me.

My whole life I tried to "be good" so people would approve of me and stick around. So I wouldn't be the little girl left in the driveway as the love of her life drove away and on to bigger and better things.

You see, there are moments in our lives that I like to call soul tattoos. They are those forever imprints that stay with you, no matter what. They can come on as sudden toxic bombs that blow your world up in a moment, or they can slowly poison you, drip by drip, until you no longer recognize yourself and wonder why you feel horrible day after day.

Mine was a toxic bomb that I was too young to recognize. It has taken me 40+ years to learn that there's a term used to describe what I experienced that day on the driveway as my dad drove away and I walked into an empty house and it's called "abandonment" and I suffered from fear of it.

It was easier for me to stay in an environment that was literally killing me, than to face the fear of being left alone again.

For years, I would tell my sons "this is not what a healthy relationship looks like" and go back to business as usual. What kind of mental mind games was I teaching them? What kind of self-worth was I instilling in them if I had none of my own?

I would pray to God to change my husband's heart because I knew I didn't deserve to be treated the way I was treated on a daily basis. I also didn't feel I deserved anything that I didn't work for, so I would try harder, do more, be better, and maybe, just maybe, then I would have earned the right to deserve to be treated better.

I would fall to my knees and cry in the shower because that was my safe space and I would just plead to my G.O.D. to please please please make things better. Please change my husband's heart so he could love me more.

I just wanted to be happy,

...and you know what happened? God did change his heart, but he had a heart attack and died.

At 49 years old, my husband died on Christmas Eve and I will never truly understand it all.

What I do know, and that I share with you here is this...

1. Be intentional and specific with your prayers because God is listening

2. You don't cause bad things to happen. Bad things happen and how you deal with them is what makes the difference in your life

3. Life isn't fair and it isn't unfair. Life is simply constant movement forward and it's full of opportunities. It's up to you to take advantage of them or not

4. God will give you ideas and images in your mind and feelings in your gut so pay attention because He's telling you something

5. You don't earn points for doing good in God's eyes and you don't get points taken away for making mistakes

I've said it before and I'll say it again, God does not make mistakes and He also does not let things go to waste.

I stepped into a toxic relationship, knowing full well, it was flashing with bright red flags all around it, but I didn't care.

My dad, my first love, had just died from cancer and I was immediately taken back to being the little girl left alone on the driveway. I was scared. I was alone. I was hurting, and I stayed quiet.

I trusted the man I was with, and even though I could see everything that was wrong with our relationship, I believed I could love him enough to make him love me just a little bit more…and that was enough.

I honestly believe God knew my spirit would be destroyed by my loyalty. I truly feel God knew I had built an endurance to pain that would allow me to continue to go through mistreatment for the sake of not giving up. I know God knew I would not leave.

God has placed a mighty calling on my life and in order for me to become the person He created me to be, and serve in the capacity He has ordered me to serve, and to be the bright light He is placing in the midst of darkness all around, I had to go through the excruciating pain of becoming a widow and losing everything, including my dignity, confidence, and self-esteem.

I am not afraid of the wound any longer.

I ripped the band-aid off because healing needed to take place and that doesn't happen by accident. All wounds need to breathe to heal, even the ones we can't physically see.

I love living in my Go Mode today because I am no longer hiding. God will do incredible things through you if you simply allow Him.

Today is the day to take action, even if it is simply ripping off the band-aid. You'll be fine and it will all make sense someday. Simply begin...

Let God Love You and Let God Heal You.

PRAYERS FROM ELENA:

As I share this piece of my heart, I simply want to pray over you.

Lord Jesus, may you heal the hearts that hurt and may you pour your love over any sadness or loneliness that remains. Let the sound of laughter and cheer fill the homes of families all around. Allow abundance to flow through each person reading this and replace their worry and stress with excitement in anticipation of your blessings that are being delivered at this very moment.

In your name...
Amen

CHAPTER 12

SECRET WITHIN

SURRENDER to RISE
R-Rise

Chapter written by Tish Ross

Acknowledgements: First, I would like to thank God for being with my children and I every step of the way. His Word says, "In this World we will have Trouble, But for us to take heart, for He has overcome the World."

Second, I want to thank my children, Tristyn and Caroline for being two of the greatest people I have the blessing of knowing and loving.

I also want to thank Elena Rodriguez, who partnered with God to guide me through the process of moving through some of my personal fears. In the words of Elena Rodriguez, "Do it afraid, Tish." "You've got this." And I did!

And finally I want to acknowledge you, the reader. Thank you for reading this book. I hope it encourages and blesses you. My name is Tish Ross. I know who I am. I know whose I am. I am stepped forward and passing my crown to you. I dedicate my chapter to you. Go Queen Go.

---

t's normal and perfectly fine to hit rock bottom. But now it is time to RISE

HOW THE HELL did I get here? I asked myself. Not just that morning as I lay on the couch fully clothed, alone with a pretty good headache. I opened my eyes and thought WTF?

How did I get here?? In this place, a place that I once called home. A handsome husband, 2 children, a boy & a girl and a dog....

Alone abandoned.

I had nothing....

I was once a stay at home mom. Not the perfect family by no means. But I was able to be at home with my children and not worry if they were being mistreated by someone else, or abused, or worse molested by a stranger or strangers. Thank God.

I am not an, "It all started when" type gal.....

Or an, "Oh Woe Is Me" chick...

But I need to tell you how I grew up. I think it is important for us as women,to dig into our past, not to get stuck there or to blame others. But as we begin to peel the layers on our journey of becoming who the hell we are really created to be. Or maybe it is trying to figure out..." Why are we the way we are?

I am grateful for self realization and the ah-ha moments. But then comes the HARD work to undo, unlearn, unbelieve some of the jacked up things that I did about myself. Sometimes this transformation is not a chosen path initially or voluntary, sometimes it is forced upon you. Let me explain..

My parents are the most beautiful people I have ever known and love. My mom was a saint and my dad, well my dad needed a little help. Unfortunately, he was a functioning and at times, depending on his mood, a raging alcoholic. He was a Navy man. A perfectionist. A genius.....A tough environment for an imperfect child to live in. We grew up in the era where children were seen and not heard. We were taught that it was wrong to ask for anything...anything at all.. WE were told when we arrived at our family's home, our AUNT & UNCLES house to NOT ASK FOR ANYTHING!! NOTHING TO DRINK, NOTHING TO EAT AND BY GOLLY DO NOT ASK TO USE THE BATHROOM!! This I believe is what planted the seed to my being extremely prideful as an adult to never ask for any kind of help. On the flipside it instilled major independence. Which I absolutely needed. So, Thanks Dad!!

Children listen, watch and learn. By watching, I learned that birthdays, anniversaries, graduations, valentines day, awards day, barbecue's, oh and the weekends were times to relax and celebrate, party rather.

I was 19 years old when a neighbor asked me to apply for the dental assistant position where she worked. Wait? Who Me? But I haven't gone to school for that? She said the dentist would train me.

I got the job, and was making really good money for a kid. I saved enough money to buy myself my very first brand spanking new car. It was a 1987 red Ford Focus. I didn't know how to drive a stick shift, but boy I bought one. And I drove it home, highways and all. Time to CELEBRATE!! I was definitely not a drinker, but I celebrated like the best of them. I just bought my first car and learned how to drive a stick on a Thursday. So that Friday, the weekend. I celebrated. And I landed in the middle of the highway. I was told that my car flipped twice and landed the wrong way on I-20. My parents were told that if I made it I would be in a vegetative or handicapped state. 475 stitches in my face and head, a broken nose, knocked out teeth and an insanely swollen arm from being laid in a bed of fire ants after being pulled from the wreckage. I woke up 3 days later in the hospital. Not allowed to look in the mirror, I should have known something was wrong when a friend of mine fainted and another had to walk out of the room as she became nauseous after seeing me.

Everyday for 33 years I looked in the mirror and heard loud and clear, You are Ugly. No one will ever listen to you.

Fast forward to 1993... I met the most handsome man who actually liked me. I met him at a bar..maybe he was drunk? Nope, he called me and asked me out. One thing led to another and in 1994 we got hitched! In 1995 I had our son and in 2000 I had our daughter. I was blessed to stay home to raise our children. WE struggled a lot financially, but at least I was home with my babies.

On May 27th, 2003 my best friend in this world, my mom, passed away. (Listen, I could go into all the ways that I grieved but I will save that for my next book. It's a lot...) One week later my dad told us kids that he didn't want to see us anymore because we reminded him too much of our mom, his wife. God told me to respect my father's wishes as he was grieving the loss of HIS soulmate, the love of his life, his wife. So I did.. Unfortunately, the worst was yet to come.

The second week in June of 2003, I walked into the house after taking my then 3 yr old daughter for a stroll around the block. By then my son was 7 yrs old and in school. I went to the phone and checked the messages. One of them changed the trajectory of our lives, family members' lives and relationships forever and ever. It was a call from CPS, Child Protective Services. I called CPS and the news I received dropped me to my knees.

I found out that a family member had been molested by my husband. I honestly have no words to describe how sickened I was, how horrible I felt for my family. I had no clue that the man that I thought I would be married to forever was a child molestor. How did this happen?! When? Where? Why? CPS then wanted to interview and observe my two children. Oh My God!! Have my children been molested by their own father??!! The family member whose child was molested, no longer wanted to have any contact or a relationship with me. The devastation that surrounded me and my children & my family was more than I could handle. I just lost my mom 2 weeks prior & my dad no longer wanted to see any of his children because of the way he was grieving. Then I lost a family member because of what my husband did. The man that I married was not at all the man that I thought I knew. I was devastated on so many levels. Then the police told me that if I could get him to confess then I needed to call them and CPS and turn him in.

Weeks later, I somehow managed to get him to confess and as soon as he did, I turned him in and lost the man that I once loved. A man that I guess I didn't really know. You have no idea the emotional, physical and mental stress that I was going through. How does one handle all of this?

Overnight without warning my children lost their dad. And I went from being a stay at home mom to a single mom. No job. No car. No child support. NOTHING and no one to help me.

Or was there?

My husband had my car towed. So, the children and I walked everywhere alone. To the laundry mat, to the store, to a friend's house, to school. EVERYWHERE. How was I supposed to find a job without a car and afford childcare? I had a mortgage payment to make so that the house wasn't another thing ripped from my children's sense of normalcy. My husband only helped with child support for approximately 3 months.

One day when my daughter and I walked to pick up my son from school there was an acquaintance standing outside waiting for her daughter to come out from the school building. We made small talk and she mentioned they were hiring part time at the gym she was working at and that I should apply. I applied, was hired on the spot and I managed to get rides to work until people got tired of having to drive me to and from work. I don't blame them, it was a 25 minute drive, and they had their own lives to live.

In the meantime I was having garage sales to pay the mortgage, pawning things to keep the water on, playing camp when the electricity was shut off, walking around the block looking for pennies to roll for lunch money and praying.

I got a ride to a local church one Sunday. Something that I do not do is walk inside big buildings not knowing ANYONE. Remember, I AM AN INTROVERT!! But God… He led and carried me and my children there. The door greeter was an older gentleman. He smiled at my children and me and said, "Welcome!!" "I am so glad that you are here!" "How are you doing this morning?"

I suddenly became overwhelmed with emotion. No one has asked me how I was doing? No one knew what my ex had done. It was a secret that I held within for decades. I didn't tell my children until they were 19 & 23 yrs in age. I couldn't. They didn't deserve that. And the Lord had whispered in my ear, "Do Not tell them what their father has done." "It will change the trajectory of their lives if you do." He also told me to not speak negatively of their father. Because his actions will speak volumes. So I listened to the Lord and I am grateful that I did. IT WAS NOT EASY!! But God...

The children and I would continue to pray on our knees and ask God to please help us with transportation. No matter what it looked like. A bus? A taxi? A job within walking distance. Something. Anything.

After wearing out my rides to work, It was about 3 days before I was going to turn in my resignation at the gym. I had no way to get there. Right before I was going to call my boss, the phone rang and it was the church I had visited a few times. The pastor on the other end of the line asked, "Tish?" "Is this Tish?" Yes, I said. It is she. He said, I have some good news for you. Our Cars for Christ program has a car for you and your children. What?!! Praise God!!

You can believe this or not... but I have absolutely no recollection of ever sharing with anyone that I needed a car. But a few months prior to this call, I was told to write a letter to the Cars for Christ Ministry telling them about my situation. I had no idea that this church existed. I had no idea that this church had this ministry. But God...

I went to pick up the car. These cars are donated by loving people. I picked up the keys and drove it to the school to pick up my son. My daughter was at my neighbors house while I did all of the running around to get insurance and then pick up the car. My car was a green 1990 Beretta. No AC but it was a car!! A huge blessing!! I went to pick up my son and when he saw the car he ran down the sidewalk and in his 8 yr old voice he yelled, "Mommy, God answered our prayers!!" My son is a youth pastor now.

I worked so hard. I ended up selling my house for $1. Yep one dollar. I had to. It had a lot of repairs so I sold it as is. And moved in with my brother into our parents house. My dad passed away and left the home to my brother and me. But God...

Years and Years later, I met my now husband. And He truly is a gift from the Lord. I did not want to date or marry. I really didn't have time to. But we met literally through a prayer request. Dated and married years later. Our family blended. My husband's son Benjamin and my two children became our focus and our life.

I started tossing and turning and when that happens I know that the Lord is trying to talk to me and tell me what He needs for me to do. I am an introvert. But I kept hearing about doing a blog. Do a podcast. Write a book. WHAT ARE YOU SAYING TO ME RIGHT NOW?!! I AM AN INTROVERT!! YOU KNOW THAT YOU DESIGNED AND CREATED ME. I cannot. But God continued to nudge me. I continued to hear Him speak. He said things like I need you to do a podcast or YouTube and interview women who have lost their sons. Specifically sons. WHAT??!! I cannot do that. Remember, I look in the mirror everyday, I am ugly. No one is going to listen to me!!

I happened upon a post on Facebook from a lady that I did not know from Adam. It read something to the effect of, "Do you want to start your own business or are You wanting to do something new in your life but you are stuck? You don't even know where to begin?" If so, message me. Remember I told you that I AM AN INTROVERT!! But ok, I'll message her. But God…

Elena Rodriguez came into my life and partnered with God to get me ready for something epic. Something bigger than what I ever imagined. Actually… I never imagined. But God…

Let me tell you this, had I not followed HIS Direction, HIS nudges, I would not be sharing this in this book.

I got connected with Elena, my life coach and she helped me make moves, take initiatives, risks on things I never would have. I had started tossing and turning again. And God asked me to start digging into research on what to ask and what not to ask mothers who have lost their sons. He wanted me to do this podcast. So I started doing this research. I found 5 women, friends of mine who have lost their son. And on Friday, September 28 of 2018 the Lord said, "Tish if you want to honor me and bring me the glory, You need to get serious and do more research right now!" So I did.

I got off from work at noon on that day.. Went home and saw a card in my door. It was from the police department of the town where my husband and I lived. It had written on it to call the Abilene police department. Our beautiful son Benjamin lived in Abilene. He lived in a sober living facility there. He was clean and sober for a year. I called my husband and told him about the card and that I would call the PD. 100 % of the time my husband would make these calls. You see, Benjamin was my husband's only biological child. He was my bonus child and 25 yrs old at this time. And since I was home from work and most of the calls we would get prior to Ben getting clean, were calls that he was in jail for one reason or another. I called and was told that our son Benjamin and his girlfriend were found deceased in a ditch that morning. It was a motorcycle accident and they were killed instantly. The grief my husband and I went through is also another hard long story. Maybe one day I will write about it. You see, the research for the podcast was not all about me. It was so that I could be semi prepared to hold and help my husband through the worst time in his life. Benjamin was his only biological son. The toxicology reports found him clean and sober. The cause of the accident was the road was dimly lit and that he over corrected and hit a utility pole. But God…

With my life coaches guidance and push, I started my podcast. It was audio only, because I didn't want anyone to see my face, but I started it. I shared my life experiences of being so afraid of my father when he was drunk and in a rage and beating us. My first episode was called, I peed in a closet. I literally did. I was hiding in the closet with my eldest sister one night, my dad was banging on our bedroom door and we hid. I told her I needed to go to the bathroom but she kept me safe in the closet and told me that it was ok to pee in there. That she would clean it up. So I did..

I went through the isolation brought on by covid like everyone else did. While there were many tragic losses of life, jobs, businesses and homes and I do not minimize that AT ALL. I was going through some solitude with the Lord. I had some come to Jesus meetings with Him. There is more detail, but let me say this, He helped me break the chains I kept myself in. I no longer look in the mirror and see ugly. I was free!! And HE told me the reason HE wanted me to do this podcast was to share with anyone, everyone that would listen to what HE has done for me. So that others will know that HE is Good!

I shared this news, this breakthrough with Elena and told her I was ready to share this news on Facebook live. She held me accountable like an excellent life coach should..And I went live and shared how Good God is and how I had kept myself in bondage. How HE forgave me for my drunk driving accident decades ago. It was me that couldn't forgive myself. But because of HIM and HIS mercy and love and forgiveness I have learned and forgiven myself!

That evening someone who NEVER watches Facebook lives, just so happened to be watching and listening to mine. Immediately after I finished the live, she messaged me and asked me to share my story on her radio show. I agreed to do so. And on the day of the radio show interview, during a one minute commercial break, The owner of the radio station asked me to bring my podcast to the station! WHAT??!! UMM, OKAY!! YES!! Two weeks later my podcast was on the radio!! But God...

I have been honored and privileged to meet and interview people from all over the world. People who had been homeless, drug addicts, alcoholics, molested, abandoned, abused, sex traffic survivors, and many many more.

I was on the radio for 3 ½ yrs until I was nudged to take my podcast to YouTube to reach more people. My VIDEO podcast, No Judgement Here with Tish Ross is now on YouTube and has close to 3000 subscribers!! But God...

The reason for the podcast was not my idea. It is all God. How could I keep everything that HE has done for me and my children to myself? How could I not share the Good News that HE is GOOD!! HE blessed me every step of the way so that myself and countless others could use my platform to share their personal journey without judgement.

Was this easy? HELL NO!! As I peeled the layers of the abandonment issues I was having. The abuse both physical, verbal and mental from my dad (whom by the way I forgave and Love to the moon and further). From the hell on earth that my ex husband put myself, my children and my family members through, you have no idea the hell.

But I share all of this with you because...I had a choice. One night I thought I'd drink my troubles away and numb all the feelings. But the morning I woke up hungover, I decided that I was NOT going to let what someone else chose to do to take me down with him. I didn't know what to do or how to do what? But I would be damned if someone else was going to dictate how to live this life. I did the hard work. I busted my booty. I quit a million times but stood up to fight a million and one times. I learned that it is not normal to not ask for help when you need it. And to provide help when someone needs you. I am a strong woman who isn't afraid to take on challenges.

I have my own podcast on YouTube for others to share their stories. I own a small online boutique. I am married and my husband and I have been to hell and back after we lost our son Benjamin. Yet I am still standing. I have been to the bottom of the barrel and literally scrimped and scraped to get by. But we did. And so can you. YOU CAN!

I went to therapy, I asked for help, I prayed on my knees and continue to get on my knees and pray daily. Now, God and I have our own personal relationship. I am quite certain that HE rolls HIS eyes at me sometimes because I still screw up. But I know that I have NEVER BEEN ABANDONED. HE HAS ALWAYS BEEN HERE WITH MY CHILDREN AND ME. WE MADE IT AND SO CAN YOU!! I promise.

Let's go. It's normal and perfectly fine to hit rock bottom. But now it is time to RISE.

This is dedicated to you. My fellow bad asses.

Peace,

Tish Ross

PRAYERS FROM ELENA:

As Tish shared the power of God showing up time and time again in our lives, she's an amazing testimony of what it means to rise again. You would never know by meeting Tish that she has endured so much pain, but what you will receive in her presence is the Power of God and that is beautiful.

Lord Jesus, may you continue to use Tish as a vessel to share your love and do your work. Keep her and her family wrapped in your loving arms and remain a constant source of acceptance as she helps others share their stories of impact. May you give all those who need courage to "do it afraid" the purpose that matters most…to do your work, and may you bring a tribe of supporters together to speak of the goodness of your love and grace.

In your name…
Amen

CONCLUSION

WALK IN FAITH

As you have read incredible stories full of hope and inspiration, I pray you feel refueled and reminded of the amazing powerhouse you are and that things can and will get better. I also want to share with you why I feel it's so important to walk in faith daily and not just when you're feeling great and happily skipping along counting your joyous blessings, but also when you feel like your body is dying inside and all you can do is trust God's Healing Hands to touch you.

Walking in Faith daily prepares you for the difficult moments that are yet to come...because they will come. It guarantees that no matter how difficult the task at hand, you are strong enough to see it through...because you are.

Walking in Faith is knowing you may have to detour, but you will get to where you're going and it will be right on time.

It is understanding your very next step may be choosing to stand still and that is moving far enough.

Never fear what's ahead when you are living true to yourself and allowing God to love you.

Often we make mistakes we are ashamed of and make choices we aren't proud of and we begin to hide and dim our own light. We begin to pick and choose the things we talk to God about as if He doesn't already know and see every single one of our faults.

The moment we open ourselves completely to God's love is the moment we can no longer hide, not even from ourselves, and it's not always easy, but it's beautiful. In fact the moment you begin to feel God's love amongst all your imperfections, something magical happens and it's as if your light begins to illuminate from within, and it's as if your whole world, and everything and everyone in it, shines brighter.

Not everyone will see your light and not everyone is meant to. Not everyone will appreciate you, value you, or even like you, and that's ok because your G.O.D. loves you and that is all that truly matters.

Only until you fall deeply in love with your G.O.D. will you understand the power of being led and guided by the one and only true leader, and fear will no longer paralyze you. The one and only source of all and everything is LOVE...and God is love.

There are moments I wish I could bottle up LOVE and give it to everyone, but I can't, and so instead I will continue to share my words and my smile.

If you are feeling lost, forgotten, or invisible, please know this...I SEE YOU AND YOU ARE ABSOLUTELY MAGNIFICENT!

So, if you are feeling lost and defeated or even like a failure...please just pause for a moment and realize that you are doing an amazing job and you are so needed. You just keep going and I promise it will get better.

Understand we're all navigating blindly because as much as we like to think we're in control, we are not. True power comes from surrendering and releasing the false belief of control.

Be mindful of your thoughts. Do your best with a spirit of excellence unto Him. Be Kind. Honest. Humble. Genuine. Honor yourself for the hot mess you are, and most importantly, Let God Love You!

I want to Thank You for sharing your time with us as we shared words of hope, inspiration, wisdom, love, and encouragement.

Welcome to the #1 Tribe of Comeback Queens who love and pray over one another and who help you to ...REMEMBER WHO YOU ARE!

Printed in the USA
CPSIA information can be obtained
at www.ICGtesting.com
JSHW080931030524
62335JS00003B/14

9 781662 893537